THE LAWS OF THE SUN

The Laws of the Sun

The Revelation of Buddha that Enlightens the New Age

by
Ryuho Okawa

The Institute for Research in Human Happiness

TABLE
OF
CONTENTS

Preface to the English Edition

With the coming of the 1990's, humankind is now poised at a great historical turning point. And particularly, the Marxist political systems of the Socialist countries are now forced to change fundamentally. As a result of a large-scale experiment with materialistic civilization, those countries must now compensate for their Godless politics.

At the same time, people in Japan, the United States and other countries of free enterprise, now seek to restore the "Age of Mind," realizing that it is impossible to break the deadlock of a materialistic culture. Certainly, it is not economics that truly liberates human beings. Genuine freedom can be achieved only through the emancipation of intrinsic human spirituality.

This book, *The Laws of the Sun*, reveals what God truly is to people of this Godless age, and stresses that the "Mind Revolution" of each individual is essential for the construction of a new civilization. This is the Genesis of our time, the Scripture for the new age and the true history book of humankind. I believe this new thought which fuses Christianity and Buddhism will save humankind at the end of this century and serve as a guide to the new age.

Written through revelations from the higher dimensional worlds, this book will light the torch of hope in the hearts of people all over the world.

Ryuho Okawa
Tokyo
May, 1990

Chapter I
When the Sun Rises
●

When the Sun Rises

•

1. The Sun of God's Truth

GOD'S TRUTH is a term which represents God's Mind, God's Law and the ever transforming Life of God. It also means a single golden thread which weaves through the past, present and future of humankind.

The golden thread of Truth has been woven, throughout human history, into a great variety of fabrics to warmly clothe people's minds. One such fabric was the Ten Commandments of Moses and another was called the Teaching of Love by Jesus Christ. From other periods were the Teachings of Shakyamuni, which were woven in India and the Teachings of Confucius, who was born in China.

However, the fabrics were not only woven two or three thousand years ago. From ancient to modern times, such fabrics of various sizes have been constantly given to this world. In Christianity, the Reformation

7

led by Martin Luther, John Calvin and others, was one fabric. And the recent emergence of a number of new, Christianity related religions is another example.

In Buddhism, not to mention the activities of highly regarded priests in China, the fabric of God's Truth was woven in Japan in the form of the development of Buddhism in the Heian Period by Saicho and Kukai (794 AD—1191 AD), and Buddhism's resurgence led by Nichiren, Honen, Shinran, Eisai, Dogen, Myoe and Ippen in the Kamakura Period (1192AD—1333AD). The same can be said about the rejuvenation of the Jodo-Shinshu sect by Rennyo in the Muromachi Period (1338AD—1573AD) and the currently active "third religious boom" in contemporary Japan.

Thus, God shrouds the minds of people with warm clothes of various colors to protect them from the materialistic and fugitive thoughts which lead them to believe that life exists only in this world. God is the great benefactor who keeps the Sun, namely God's Truth, shining to supply heat and light to brighten people's minds.

The Sun of God's Truth has been constantly providing unlimited light energy to humankind. Indeed, it has always been above, shining ever so brilliantly!

Occasionally, however, as clouds blocked the sunlight, rain fell and the cold winds frightened the rain-drenched people, the Sun of God's Truth seemed to have disappeared in silence for a long period of time.

Nevertheless, beyond an endless sea of clouds exists the noble sun, forever radiating its golden light.

Therefore, whenever the light of God's Truth seems to disappear from this world due to the confusion created in human minds, a golden ray will eventually come out from behind the thick clouds.

This very light is the light of salvation and the light of life which delivers people from the age of darkness.

The Laws of the Sun, which I will now reveal, shall describe the rising of the Sun of Truth with words of truth. It once seemed to have set, but after an interlude of some two thousand years, it is rising again from the horizon as a far greater light than ever. This Law shall give hope to people of today and leave behind a golden treasure to people of the future.

As the Sun of God's Truth gradually rises, a great light will glow from a corner of the earth. This very corner is the chosen land, Japan. Therefore, many people will hereafter see the Sun of God's Truth rising slowly and radiantly from Japan as the focal point. The world is craving this light now. There is a crying need for God's Truth to pervade the world with the power of the rising sun, to shatter the fortress of darkness named "delusion" which humankind has long been building.

I am writing this book, *The Laws of the Sun*, because it is my desire that as many of you as possible take part in spreading God's Truth throughout the world as a noble achievement in your life.

I will fill each and every word with my earnest prayers to save the world. I wish for every one of those words to become that of life, that of light, and be cherished by all brothers and sisters of this earth.

2. What is God?

Living on the earth, in this three-dimensional world, have you ever deeply contemplated the truth of your "Life"? If you have, what conclusions have you reached? For our reflections on life let us start by defining life.

You may think that life is only a matter of decades on the earth; from the birth of a human being to his death. If you do, your idea of life will change completely as you read this book.

If life is finite, and if when a particular person carrying a given name dies, nothing is left but a handful of ash and bones, not even good enough to feed a dog, and the rest spreads into the air as carbon dioxide gas, why should we struggle through our lives? For what reason should we study and toil? And for what purpose have we been refining our idea of life or chasing a dream?

The teachings of Gautama Buddha, or Shakyamuni, which were taught two thousand five hundred and several tens of years ago in India; were these completely false? The meanings and the mission of life which he taught throughout his eighty years of life, and his theory that the other world, or the Real World exists; was all this false and meant to mislead people? I must say that they were not. These were not theories conceived by immature people.

Those who boast of being intellectuals in the modern age, which of you has mastered and conquered the truth well enough to contradict Shakyamuni?

If you say that Shakyamuni's teachings were utterly false, can you insist that God's Truth taught by Jesus Christ two thousand years ago was also a lie? The "God" that Jesus Christ believed in, whom billions of people from all over the world have never ceased to respect; is it just an empty theory based on Jesus' self-righteous and distorted thoughts? The truthful envoy of God, having prayed with a sweat of blood in Gethsemane and then crucified while wearing a crown of thorns; the person who dismisses Jesus as crazy is the one who must prove himself sane in the eyes of the world.

I declare to any "scientific rationalist" who maintains that he would believe in God if he saw proof that, "You should only speak after you take off your hat and bow to Moses, Shakyamuni, and Jesus Christ. These are the great figures that humankind has exalted for thousands of years of history" and, "You had better prove that you are more perfect than these figures whose teachings have warranted 'respect' for thousands of years."

No one is able to do such a thing because nobody has mastered God's Truth as thoroughly as Moses, Shakyamuni or Jesus Christ.

It doesn't do any harm to pursue the proof of God's

existence, out of personal curiosity. However, it is premature to proclaim whether God exists or not, based on one's own findings. Without learning how much humankind has reflected on, believed in and understood God, it is hasty to draw conclusions.

Therefore, let us begin to study "What is God?" humbly and open-heartedly. This is a truly scientific and positive approach.

At some point in the course of research into your life, you can never avoid encountering the existence of God as you are constantly given hints of his existence. Birth and death are the most important keys. But at the time of an illness, love or a failure, you may also catch a glimpse of God.

I intend to answer the question, "What is God?" throughout this book. In the meantime, I will present to you many hints on and solutions to "the purpose and mission of life."

3. Existence and Time

Humankind, since its birth on earth, has beheld the existence of all living things and all things great and small under the radiantly shining sun. We must acknowledge that there exists a universal rule, or truth ; it is the law of transmutation. Every living creature on earth, no matter whether it is a human, an animal, a plant, a mineral or microorganism, is under the law of transmutation.

Then, what is the law of transmutation ? It means that every single "thing" on earth has a period of birth, growth, decline and extinction. For example, this law applies to human beings as we are born, grow up, become old and finally die.

The law is relevant to every "thing," whether it is natural or artificial. For instance, take a car. A car has a period of production and another of efficient and reliable service. Eventually, it will break down and finally be scrapped. The same can be said of a plant. When you plant a seed, it sprouts, grows and blooms. After it flowers, it will wither and disappear completely from the ground, leaving behind only seeds or a bulb.

Thus, every single being in this three-dimensional world goes through four phases : birth or an origin, growth or full operation, decline or disorder and death or dissolution.

Simply, every being in this three-dimensional, phenomenal world comprehends the time of transformation and, therefore, nothing is stagnant. It can also be said that every thing is permitted to "exist" on condition that it transforms.

Moreover, an "existence" in this world, destined to transform or transmute, can be likened to a film which is projected by time, which acts as a projector. The existence embraces a quality which allows it to transmute. To explain that more simply, every single "being" in this world changes every moment and cannot remain in exactly the same condition. For example, the cells of your body are not in the same condition when compared with their state of yesterday.

However, there exists an entity which governs the entire physical body even though it is comprised of constantly changing cells. There is "something" which never changes behind an existence that keeps on transforming in the current of time for a human, an animal and a plant.

For example, what makes a plant a certain flower and not a random collection of vegetal cells? If a group of coincidentally assembled plant cells form a particular flower on a particular day, the flower should transform into something else but a flower, according to the law of transmutation.

However, a flower is just a flower. Yesterday it was a flower. Today, it is a flower. And tomorrow it will be a flower. It cannot become anything but a flower. It only changes its condition as a flower. Also, a chrysanthemum never changes into a tulip; a tulip never changes into a cosmos. A tulip will finish its life as a tulip.

There is "something" which never changes during a change. There is "something" which never transmutes during a transmutation. That "something" is sometimes referred to as "Real Existence," and at other times as a "concept," or as an "idea."

The famous saying in Buddhism, "Matter is void and void is matter," is true. We understand that there exists something unchangeable within a change, and that a universal existence is projected to be a material existence which transmutes. We do not regard a human being as merely a collection of fragile cells that are perpetually changing. The essence of a human being is not something transient which perpetually transforms in the current of time, but an eternally unchangeable entity. This unchanging entity is life, the soul or the spirit.

By the word, "spirit," I do not mean a peculiar, extraordinary phenomenon. It is the essence of a human being, the unchangeable entity, and the idea of life ; an intelligence with a personality which governs a material human body. It is a consciousness with a personality which allows a human, as matter, to exist. This is the essence of a human being. No matter what impression people might have of the word spirit, there is only one Truth ; a flower has its own life, as does a human being.

4. The Finite and the Infinite

I have mentioned the subject of "time" in the previous section. Also, I referred briefly to the matter of existence. Now I would like to tell you about what is beyond "time" and "existence"; namely, the "finite" and the "infinite."

Whether a life is finite or infinite ; it is a question every human being comes across at least once.

Before drawing any conclusion, I would like to

present to you a story.

Once upon a time, there was a big turtle. It took him ten minutes to step forward with his right foreleg, another ten minutes to step forward with his left foreleg, and another ten minutes for each of his hindlegs. Thus, it took him forty minutes to move one pace. One day this turtle wondered whether there was an end to the sandy beach and decided to explore the world. He looked to the furthermost point of the beach and started to walk with all his strength.

The turtle reasoned that it took him forty minutes to advance one pace and decided to leave his footprints in the sand to avoid retracing his steps. Don't you think he was wise ?

However, one day, without completing his quest to reach the end of the coastline, he was entirely exhausted. He died believing that he had conquered at least half of the world.

The next day a fisherman came along, dragged the turtle to the other side of the island and ate him. Did it take the fisherman a long time to cross the island ? No, it took him only ten minutes, given his fast pace.

As a matter of fact, the poor turtle only walked around and around the sandy beach of the small island, without knowing that waves from the Pacific Ocean were mercilessly erasing his footprints.

When contemplating the finite and the infinite, I cannot help recalling this story. What is the difference between the turtle and the fisherman ? Walking speed ? Body size ? The amount of experience ? You could agree with all of these facts. However, the fundamental difference between the turtle and the fisherman is the gap between their abilities to comprehend. Although the turtle's target, efforts and enthusiasm are highly commendable, his results were somewhat pathetic. Why? It is because of the apparent difference between those who understand and those who do not ; and the difference between those who see and those who do not.

Now, how about replacing the turtle and the fisherman with one who does not believe in God and one who does ? Some of you might be offended and protest at being compared with a turtle. Those who think that a life is limited to only sixty to seventy years, and that death will bring a complete end to it ; those who boast that the world is only what they can see with their eyes, and that they do not believe in a world beyond their five senses ; they are doing nothing but merely walking around and around within their small and limited world, just like that turtle on his adventure, depending upon their footprints as the only guide. I really sympathize with such people. Moreover, as they toil through life in a sweat, and tread their way around a small island, just like that turtle, those people look somewhat pathetic.

We human beings have been living eternal lives for eons and have reincarnated many times over on the earth to experience spiritual training in life.

As human lives are not limited to this three-dimensional world on the terrestrial ground, let us look for a moment at the magnetic field surrounding the earth. We all were originally inhabitants of the World of Real Existence (the Real World), or the worlds starting from the fourth dimension. The universe extends into the five-dimensional, six-dimensional, seven-dimensional, eight-dimensional, nine-dimensional and the ten-dimensional worlds. Human lives live in differently harmonized realms in accordance with the grades of their souls.

Therefore, I must ask those who seriously question whether or not the universe is finite, "Is your universe three-dimensional, or is it the multi-dimensional universe starting from the fourth dimension?"

If the universe is compared to the human body, the three-dimensional universe would be a naked body. The four-dimensional universe would be like an undergarment over the naked body. Likewise, you can make comparisons as follows: the fifth dimension—a shirt over an undergarment; the sixth dimension—a sweater over a shirt; the seventh dimension—a suit over a sweater; the eighth dimension, a coat to wrap around the body; and the ninth dimension, a hat on the head.

The above is only a simile, but illustrates very well the structure of the multi-dimensional universe. Thus, higher dimensions can be described as those which contain lower dimensions within them. They may be similar, but they have higher objectives than their lower counterparts.

5. Multi-Dimensional Universe

In the previous section I explained the multi-dimensional universe using the illustration of a human body clothed by various garments. However, here I would like to give a more logical explanation of the multi-dimensional world.

We often say we are in the three-dimensional world, but what exactly is meant by "three dimensions"?

Dimension is a term used to describe the various essential elements that make up a given world.

For instance, the first dimension consists of a straight line, which is a continuation of points. Assuming there were inhabitants of the first dimension, the method used to distinguish each other would be the length of segments, or whether oneself is longer or shorter than another. Therefore, if the length of two inhabitants were the same, it would be impossible to tell the two apart.

By contrast, the second dimension consists of length and width. Length and width define a particular surface or plane. Therefore, if there were inhabitants in this world, they would be flounder-like beings with surface but no height or depth. Accordingly, if two of these beings had the same surface area as defined by length and width, they would be indistinguishable.

Next, what about our three-dimensional world?

19

The third dimension consists of length, width and height.

What we define as length, width and height is "shape." The inhabitants of the third dimension cannot be mistaken for each other unless one has exactly the same shape as another in every respect ; the same height, the same width, and the same depth. Thus, differentiation here is more complex than in the case of the two-dimensional flounder-like beings.

In the fourth dimension, the element, time, is added to the elements, length, width, and height of the third dimension. In the third dimension, things in a particular space always share the same time. This is not the case in the fourth dimension. Simply, in the third dimension, the people with whom we shake hands, or the objects we touch always exist with us at the same time, at a particular time, on a particular day, in a particular month of a particular year. This is not the case in the fourth dimension.

In the case of the inhabitants of the fourth dimension, the people who are shaking hands are not always of the same period. A person from the Kamakura Period (1192AD—1333 AD) can shake hands with another from the Showa Period (1926 AD—1989 AD). What is impossible in the third dimension can happen in the fourth. Therefore, in the fourth dimension, it is difficult to tell whether the building in front of you exists now or if you are seeing an illusion of a building of the past. Nevertheless, even though it is only an illusion, it feels as if it exists. Thus, in the fourth dimension, the time indicated by each person's watch is not always the same and a woman, for example, who once lived in the Heian Period (798AD—1185AD) can appear youthful.

The concept of the prediction can be explained in the same way. In the fourth dimension, something which would happen in the future of the third dimension can appear as if it is happening at any time.

In the fifth dimension, the element, spirituality, is added as another element in addition to length, width, height and time. These five elements define this particular world. In other words, to distinguish oneself from another, an inhabitant of the fifth dimension measures his grade of spirituality as well as comparing his shape as defined by length, width, height and time period.

The condition to live in the fifth dimension is awareness of spirituality, or the realization that a human being is not just a material body. The scale by which to measure spirituality is mainly "goodness." The fifth dimension is, therefore, where the good people collect.

In the sixth dimension, knowledge about God is involved as the sixth element in addition to length, width, height, time and spirituality. In this world, the standard by which to differentiate one from another is how much knowledge one has about God, in addition to shape, the time period and the grade of spirituality. The conditions for a life in the sixth dimension are that one must be morally good and possess much knowledge about Divinity. Of course, one's knowledge of

God differs in each person. At least, anyone who doesn't believe in God's Truth cannot exist in the sixth dimension.

6. Higher-Dimensional Universe

Now, I will explain the worlds beyond the sixth dimension.

In the seventh dimension, altruism is involved as the seventh element, in addition to the six elements of length, width, height, time, spirituality and knowledge about God. Objectively speaking, inhabitants up to the sixth dimension live self-centerdly, though not necessarily badly. Even in the highly evolved sixth dimension, people still strive to acquire knowledge of God for self-development. Essentially, the inhabitants up to the sixth dimension are like students and not yet adult members of the society. If you see a person in the sixth dimension as a university student, someone in the fifth dimension could be compared to a high school student, and the inhabitants in the fourth and third dimensions could be compared to secondary and primary school pupils, respectively.

Having reached the seventh dimension, a human is a graduate and ready to start his life as a member of society. The primary objective for the inhabitants of the seventh dimension is altruism. It can be expressed as "love," in terms of mental attitude, and "service," in terms of action. Therefore, because people belonging to the seventh dimension are providing each other with love and service, they actively guide people of and below the sixth dimension, especially people who are lost in the fourth dimension after departing from their lives in a physical body. Moreover, some seven-dimensional beings reincarnate on earth to practice lives of love and service. Thus, such respectable persons live in the seventh dimension.

In the eighth dimension, mercy is added to the seven elements of length, width, height, time, spirituality, knowledge of God and altruism. Mercy is the willingness and the ability of a higher graded person to give without reserve and discrimination ; this is mercy. If the love of the seventh dimension is expressed as the "love that gives," that of the eight-dimensional world can be expressed to be a more highly classed love, the "love that gives perpetually" or "infinite love."

While the love of the seventh dimension is still a result of human efforts, or the result of willingness to love selflessly, the worldly love of the eighth dimension is like that of the sun, or an "inexhaustible love." It is merciful love. In contrast to the love of the seventh dimension which is selective, and which varies in degree according to the love-object, the love of the eighth dimension can be expressed as one of "impartiality and probity." The inhabitants of the eighth dimension are truly qualified to be leaders because they provide infinite love with no discrimination.

In the ninth dimension, the universe is added to the

eight elements, length, width, height, time, spirituality, knowledge of God, altruism and mercy. Inhabitants of dimensions up to the eighth dimension live within a multi-dimensional universe which is a magnetic field formed in the earth's stratosphere. In contrast, the ninth dimension doesn't limit itself to the universe of the terrestrial globe, but is connected to the spiritual worlds related to other systems beyond our solar system. The inhabitants of the ninth dimension are those who guide the terrestrial spiritual group in the evolution process of the Cosmos. Most of the incarnate gods, or the fundamental divinities of world-wide religions are from the ninth dimension. It is the world where live spirits who take charge of the origin of Law.

The means of distinguishing between the inhabitants of that world lies in the color of the Light, which is the origin of Law. There is, of course, only one Law of God, but it is divided into lights of seven different colors, in accordance with the character of each inhabitant of the ninth dimension.

Above the ninth dimension exists the tenth dimension as the highest grade within the terrestrial spirit group. In this world there is no spirit who has experienced life in a human body on earth. There are only three "consciousnesses."

The original elements of the tenth dimension are creation and evolution, in addition to mercy from the eighth dimension and universe of the ninth dimension. In the tenth dimension, there are no distinctions of character as with human beings, but only differences in roles relating to creation and evolution. The three consciousnesses of the tenth dimension are called the "Grand Sun Consciousness," the "Moon Consciousness" and the "Earth Consciousness."

The Grand Sun Consciousness governs the active will; namely, the positiveness of all the terrestrial lives including humans. The Moon Consciousness governs the negative, elegant and feminine aspects. The Earth Consciousness is the consciousness of the terrestrial globe as a life form and is in charge of the Creation of Earth. The four-hundred and fifty million years of earth's history developed under the influence of these three consciousnesses.

Within the terrestrial universe, the tenth dimension is the highest. However, in the Solar system, there exists the eleventh dimension with the distinctive element of the "mission of the solar system," or the life and spiritual existence as the sun itself. Moreover, the twelve-dimensional existence is a Great Divine Spirit called "Galaxy Consciousness," which governs the project of the universe of Galaxies. It governs tens or hundreds of thousands of eleven-dimensional star consciousnesses, including the Solar Divine Spirit of our solar system (cf. a ten-dimensional existence is called "the planetary consciousness").

Although this is as far as I can see, I estimate that the Macrocosmic Grand Divine Spirit belongs to the world as high as the twentieth dimension.

7. The Birth of Life (1)
The Birth of Stars

The question, "What happens to human beings after death?" is often asked out of religious interest. Conversely, the question, "By what process have living beings, including humans, been given life?" or the mystery of the birth of life, is often asked out of scientific interest. Here I shall tell you about the birth of life. I will talk about the mystery of the origin of life with the intention to prove that both religious and scientific interest will ultimately lead to a single goal.

It is said that the very beginning of the third dimension, including the Earth on which we live, was around forty billion years ago.

If the Macrocosmic Grand Divine Spirit, or the primordial God, is as developed as a twenty-dimensional existence or higher, there has existed God as a consciousness for hundreds of billions of years, or eternally.

God intended to create the three-dimensional universe around one hundred billion years ago and created, by His own Will, a Grand Divine Spirit to govern the three-dimensional universe about eighty billion years ago. This was the origin of the thirteenth dimension and the birth of the very first Divine Spirit related to the universe.

Chapter I : When the Sun Rises

The thirteen-dimensional Cosmic Divine Spirit is a projection of the consciousness of the God of Origin, whose mission is the Creation of the Cosmos. The thirteen-dimensional Cosmic Divine Spirit created the two million nebular consciousness Divine Spirits, which belong to the twelfth dimension. The Galaxy Consciousness Divine Spirit, who governs us, is also one of these two million nebular consciousnesses.

Sixty billion years ago, the eleven-dimensional star consciousness Divine Spirits were created by the twelve-dimensional nebular consciousness Divine Spirits. This is the origin of the eleven-dimensional universe. In the case of the universe which we are a part of, the twelve-dimensional Galaxy Consciousness Divine Spirit created the eleven-dimensional Solar System Consciousness Divine Spirit.

Moreover, fifty-three billion years ago, planetary consciousness was created in the Galaxy by the eleven-dimensional star consciousness Divine Spirits. This is the origin of the ten-dimensional universe. In our solar system, the eleven-dimensional Solar System Divine Spirit gave birth to the consciousnesses of Mercury, Venus, Earth, Mars, Jupiter, Saturn and so on. The creation of such planetary consciousness Divine Spirits had been almost completed by about forty-two billion years ago.

Finally, forty billion years ago, an extraordinary event took place inside the Cosmic Divine Spirit. In other words, a series of phenomena like nuclear fusion and nuclear fission, or simply, the "Big Bang," happened inside the consciousness of the thirteen-dimensional Cosmic Divine Spirit.

Consequently, inside the thirteen-dimensional Cosmic Divine Spirit, a three dimensional space was created, which can be compared to the internal organs of a human being. Of course, it wasn't like the systematic cosmos we see now. It was as if a jellyfish-like stomach suddenly appeared. To give clarity to the jelly fish-like space, the twelve-dimensional nebular consciousnesses, the eleven-dimensional star consciousness and the ten-dimensional planetary consciousnesses collaborated to materialize a series of planets, stars and nebulae.

Since the appearance of the three-dimensional space forty billion years ago, progress in the creation of the universe varies according to each nebula and each solar system. Within this Galaxy, our solar system appeared about ten billion years ago in the three-dimensional space. Seven billion years ago Mercury was born, six billion years ago Venus was born and, four billion five hundred million years ago, the Earth was born. This is the origin of our stars. A star is also one of the original consciousnesses with life.

8. The Birth of Life (2)
The Birth of the Human Spirit and Other Lives

When was the first human spirit born into the Cosmos ? It is not clear. However, considering that the

original form of the three-dimensional space was created forty billion years ago, followed by the nebulae, the
Galaxy, the Solar system and so on, there is no doubt
that the lives of stars were first born and, based on
those models, other various forms of lives were born.

To avoid complication, I will focus on the birth of
individual lives as related to the solar system.

It was about ten billion years ago when the Sun, as
a star, emerged in the three-dimensional space. Next,
about seven billion years ago, Mercury was created.
However, it was not ready to be inhabited.

The first life was born in the solar system after the
beautiful star Venus was created six billion years ago.
Five hundred million years later, or five billion five
hundred million years ago, it was decided that the
nine-dimensional world should be created in the solar
system. There were created highly evolved Divine
Spirits with personalities, who were more mobile than
ten-dimensional planetary consciousnesses and, therefore, more capable of governing the lives of those born
on the stars. The first nine-dimensional Divine Spirit
was named El Miore, governor of Venus.

However, at that point, the fourth dimension up to
the eighth dimension had not yet been established in
the Solar system. The lives which El Miore created in
the three-dimensional world of Venus were crosses
between plant and animal; they could not communicate with the nine-dimensional world effectively. The
first Venusian's upper body looked like a lily flower on
human legs and had leaves on its back to support its

life through photosynthesis.

El Miore created millions of Venusians but failed to achieve any significant success. These Venusians were meant to have eternal life but their spiritual training did not work effectively on the surface of Venus. They couldn't make any progress even though hundreds of thousands of years elapsed. At that time the system of transmigration had not been established because their experience on the surface of Venus was not helpful enough for the semi-plant, semi-animal Venusians to achieve the spiritual level required to live in the nine-dimensional world where El Miore belonged. In other words, as they had nowhere else to go, there was no option but to let them live eternally as Venusians.

These Venusians lived a little over four billion years or so, but most of them died because of the violent volcanic eruptions on Venus about one billion and five hundred million years ago.

Concurrent with the experiment of life on Venus, the earth was created four billion five hundred million years ago when the ten-dimensional consciousnesses of the earth were contemplating the birth of lives on the Earth's surface. Based on the failed experiment on Venus, the high spirits discussed the construction of a terrestrial life spirit group with a focus on evolution. The failure on Venus taught them that an infinite life on the ground does not stimulate evolution but leads only to stagnation.

Therefore, the three terrestrial, ten-dimensional Divine Spirits ; The Grand Sun Consciousness, the

Moon Consciousness and the Earth Consciousness decided to establish two basic policies for life activity on the terrestrial globe. The first policy was to make life on the ground multi-leveled in its manifestation. The second policy was to limit the length of activities of life on the earth, and to make the rule of transmigration between different dimensional worlds.

Based on the first policy, the Divine Spirits started, three billion years ago, to create amoebae, plankton and the like. These were the bases of animals. Two billion six hundred million years ago, the creation of fungi such as molds began. These were the bases of plants. Eventually, higher-graded lives were brought to the earth.

Based on the second policy, the Divine Spirits first created a lower graded spiritual world, which is the origin of the current four-dimensional Posthumous Realm. At that time the realm was only a vague, veil-like spiritual field covering the earth. The initial microorganisms and low-grade plants repeated their transmigration between this low-grade spiritual world and life activities on the earth.

About six hundred million years ago, the terrestrial planetary Divine Spirits recognized that the time had at last arrived to create high-grade lives on the globe. They created the nine-dimensional spiritual world on the earth and invited El Miore from Venus. El Miore was commissioned to take charge of the creation of high-grade lives represented by mammals, based on his experience of creating lives on Venus.

Then how were superior lives created ?

First, a consciousness was made in the low-grade spiritual world, with the idea, for example, to create a "mouse." Then the consciousness was placed into one of the most highly evolved animals on the ground and, through gradual alterations, finally was completed the creation of a creature called "mouse." Using the same process, rabbits, dogs, cats and so on, were created. In time, high-grade animals flourished on the earth and the system of transmigration got under way.

El Miore declared, in discussions with the ten-dimensional spirits, that the time to create humankind on the earth was near. They decided to ask for the cooperation of the nine-dimensional Divine Spirits of other stars to give birth to humankind on the earth about four hundred million years ago.

First, the nine-dimensional spirit of Sagittarius, Amor, was invited. Second, the nine-dimensional spirit from Cancer, Moria, was invited. And then the nine-dimensional spirit, Therabim, was invited from Cygnus. Preparations to create the terrestrial human spirit group proceeded through the cooperation of the nine-dimensional Divine Spirits.

At one time the governor of Venus and the very first nine-dimensional existence of the terrestrial spirit group, El Miore, changed his name to El Cantare ; it means "the Beautiful Land of Light, the Earth." El Cantare was reborn on the earth in India two thousand five hundred and some years ago at which time he was called Shakyamuni (Gautama Buddha).

Amor, from Sagittarius, was born in present-day Israel two thousand years ago as Jesus Christ. Moria, from Cancer, was called Moses when he was born in Egypt three thousand and some hundreds of years ago. Therabim, who arrived to earth fourth, from Cygnus, was born in China two thousand and several hundreds of years ago as Confucius. Thus, the initial four nine-dimensional, personal Divine Spirits dwelled on earth.

9. The Initiation of the Terrestrial Spirit Group

The four terrestrial nine-dimensional Divine Spirits, Shakyamuni, Jesus Christ, Moses and Confucius, discussed what kind of human to develop on the earth. They reached a conclusion on two fundamental points based on the previously mentioned rules of evolution ; 1) To give different levels of spiritual enlightenment to humankind so that humans will perpetually evolve ; 2) To make human life on earth finite so that humans would transmigrate between the earth and the spiritual world.

First, the creation of humankind on the ground was carried out using the spiritual life forms of those who once lived as Venusians. The process, however, limited humans to an anthropoid-level. Subsequently, it took several hundred million more years to develop a highly evolved human spirit as the nine-dimensional Divine

Spirits had intended. They then decided to invite human spirits appropriate for Earth from other highly evolved stars in order to form a highly developed terrestrial spirit group. This took place three hundred and sixty-five million years ago.

From the distant and highly evolved Planet Beta, in the Magellanic nebula, a selected group of sixty million spirits traveled to the Earth in a big fleet of space crafts under the direction of Aal El Ranty. The place where they landed is now called the banks of the Nile river in modern Egypt. This land was selected because it was a rich land, filled with greenery and water. Here was established the first Utopia because it was an ideal land and environment to live in. This is the origin of the legend of the Garden of Eden.

After the arrival of El Ranty the development and evolution of the earth accelerated. In the meantime, El Ranty left his body and returned to heaven as the fifth nine-dimensional Divine Spirit. Later he was called Allah, the God of Creation. "Allah" originated from the name, "Aal El Ranty" ; he had mainly acted as the God of Evolution up to this point.

Ever since El Ranty returned to heaven, other people who were living in Eden on the ground left their bodies and returned to heaven one after another. Consequently, there arose a need to create realms suitable to these peoples' different spiritual levels. Thus, the eighth dimension, "Diamond Realm" ("Nyorai Realm"), the seventh dimension, "Sacred Heavenly Realm" ("Bosatsu Realm") and the sixth dimension,

"Godly Realm," were created around the earth.

The initial inhabitants of the eighth dimension, "Nyorai Realm," were seven Archangels who were brought along by El Ranty. They were Micha, Gabri, Rapha, Sali, Uri, Lagu and Luci. These seven Archangels were granted the title "El," meaning, "The Light of God," as a reward for establishing the Garden of Eden. Since then, they have called themselves Michael, Gabriel, Raphael, Saliel, Uriel, Laguel and Lucifel.

However, about one hundred and twenty million years ago, when he was born on the earth as Satan, one of the seven Archangels, Lucifel, was degraded because he indulged in the lust for status and fame, materialism and sensual pleasure. As he couldn't return to the eighth dimension, he rebelled and formed the Hell Realm within a low-grade spiritual world. It was the chief Archangel, Michael, who confined Lucifel in a corner of the four-dimensional Posthumous Realm and left him without a supply of heat and light. Lucifel later changed his name to Lucifer and has continued to be the·emperor of Hell for more than one hundred million years. In the "Nyorai Realm," Lucifel was replaced by Panuel as the seventh Archangel.

By three hundred and several tens of millions of years ago, the terrestrial spiritual worlds of the ninth, eighth, seventh and sixth dimension had been completed. The rest was a lower grade spiritual world. And two hundred and seventy million years ago, a huge fleet brought as many as one billion people from Orion.

Since the Earth had by then established itself as the place for spiritual trainees, the second immigration to form the terrestrial spirit group took place.

Along with this fleet came three nine-dimensional Divine Spirits; Achemene, Orgon and Kaitron. Achemene was born as "Manu" in the Middle East, where he had made the Code of Manu. Orgon was called Maitrayer Nyorai and was very active in the age of the Lemuria and the Atlantis Continent, but he has not been born on the ground for the past ten thousand years. Kaitron was called Koot Hoomy in theosophy. He is mainly in charge of scientific technology. He was born in Greece as Archimedes and was later reincarnated as Isaac Newton.

Thus, the earth's five-dimensional Spiritual Realm was created. Moreover, one hundred and thirty million years ago, the third fleet of two billion human spirits flew over from Pegasus. Along with them came the ninth and tenth nine-dimensional leaders, Theoria and Samatria, respectively. Theoria was born in Greece three thousand and several hundred years ago as Zeus. Samatria was born in Persia as Zoroaster and at another time as Mani. He was the founder of Zoroastrianism and Manichaeism.

As the ten Divine Spirits collected in the ninth dimension, the guidance system of the terrestrial spirit group was made firm. At the same time, the fourth-dimensional Posthumous Realm was being formed.

10. Expansion of the Terrestrial Spirit Group and the Appearance of Corrupt Souls

The terrestrial spirit group had expanded to approximately four billion in population by one hundred and thirty million years ago. At that time, El Ranty proposed to create new terrestrial spirits, as the combination of spirits from different stars did not have any particular character as a spirit group. El Ranty's idea was to create five branch spirits around the core of a high-grade human spirit which immigrated to the earth, and to make them live on the earth in turn for effective spiritual studies. Therefore, the nine-dimensional Divine Spirits and some others cooperated to devise a gigantic machine called "Pytron," which served to intensify God's Light. By applying the intensified light to a core spirit, five branch spirits were born.

From this, the population of the terrestrial spirit group expanded to several tens of billions. However, there arose a problem. Since many branch spirits created by means of the "Pytron" had lower spiritual grades than their originals, increasing numbers of them lost sight, in the course of their lives on the ground, of the fact that they were originally spirits and indulged in materialism or lust. And many of them began to exert evil influence over other normal spirits. After their deaths, these degraded human spirits formed a magnetic field within the lower spiritual world, and a group of spirits bearing dark intentions developed in the four-dimensional Posthumous Realm. This was the origin of the Hell Realm.

When Lucifer revolted against the high spirits in Heaven and formed Hell one hundred and twenty million years ago, a cloud formed by the evil negative energy blocked God's Light forever. Hell became a cold and dark world.

Moreover, the creation of such a world of darkness within the four-dimensional Posthumous Realm shadowed a part of the three-dimensional world on the ground and blocked God's Light. Even though the sun shines radiantly, a cloud in the sky can shadow the ground and make it cloudy. In the same way, since one hundred and twenty million years ago, all sorts of evil and chaos were brought to the third dimension on the terrestrial ground.

Since then, for more than one hundred million years, battles have constantly taken place in this three-dimensional phenomenal world, mainly between high-grade Angels of Light who are striving to purify the earth, and Hell's devils and evil spirits led by Lucifer, who want to expand their territory in the three-dimensional world to escape the agony of Hell.

This book, *The Laws of the Sun,* is being written in an effort to make God's Light shine as it did originally, to revive the Light of the Sun of God's Truth in all its splendor.

Chapter I : When the Sun Rises

My readers, when you have attained thorough com-
prehension of the previously mentioned history of the
terrestrial spirit group, please understand how sincerely
motivated I am in revealing to you the Law of the
future. *The Laws of the Sun* are the laws of salvation,
in an effort to regain the original Land of Light, the
Garden of Eden.

Chapter II
God's Truth Speaks

•

God's Truth Speaks

•

1. The Truth of the Soul

In chapter I, I discussed the Creation of the universe and the history of the formation of the terrestrial spirit group. As the process shows, so-called "Creation" is the history of higher-dimensional spirits making lower-dimensional spirits. And High Divine Spirits have been created in various dimensions in accordance with the intentions of the ultra-dimensional primordial God. Following the creation of star and planetary consciousnesses, an extraordinary event took place within the Macrocosmic Grand Divine Spirit which resulted in the origin of the three-dimensional universe. Stars and nebulae were created in the three-dimensional space, followed by the creation of each planet in each solar system of dimensions where human spirits below the ninth dimension dwell. Creation went like this:

In our solar system, the nine-dimensional Cosmic

Realm (or the Sun Realm) was first created, followed by the eight-dimensional Nyorai Realm (or the Diamond Realm), the seven-dimensional Bosatsu Realm (or the Sacred Heavenly Realm), the six-dimensional Godly Realm (or the Light Realm), the five-dimensional Spiritual Realm (or the Mental Realm) and the four-dimensional Posthumous Realm, which includes the Astral Realm and the Hell Realm (refer to the table of Dimensional Structures on page 217).

A multi-dimensional structure of realms, equivalent to those of the earth, can be found in other cosmic spaces. While the ninth dimension is connected to other star system's spirit groups, the eighth dimension and below has developed independently within each star system.

All those make it clear that an individual life, called a soul, is the manifestation, at lower levels, of the ultra-high-dimensional primordial God. God is not a being who exists outside us, but a very high-dimensional consciousness which allows us to exist. Therefore, we are a part of God's consciousness and a form of God's self expression.

In other words, God created the Macrocosms, and lives within it, as a way to express himself. These are the projections of God's consciousness. Accordingly, if God should one day wish to terminate the existence of the Macrocosms, this apparently infinite three-dimensional universe would suddenly disappear. Needless to say, our individual life forms as humans, because they are mere transient existences, would disappear completely if God should abandon His Will to express Himself. However, it is possible for our transient, individual lives to be extremely high-grade existences because they are a part of God's consciousness.

Therefore, we must be proud and confident that we are a part of God, and take part in His self-expression. This is the truth of the soul. Past religions and advanced philosophies have been handed down and developed to make earthly people recognize this truth. The ultimate objective of natural and space science, which are developing remarkably, is also to reveal this truth of the soul.

Based on the wonderful truth of the soul, that we are a part of the Consciousness of the great God, I wish to discuss the ideal state of the soul and the ideal state of life as a human being. I am sure that the Truth will reveal Itself in due course.

2. The Nature of the Soul

Now, what is the nature of our souls, which are said to be a part of God ? The nature and character of God will be revealed by our research into the nature of our souls.

Soul has several distinctive features, the first of which is creativity. Soul is endowed with the ability to transform itself in any way at will. In other words, it can decide what sorts of thoughts it will have as a consciousness.

For instance, it can manifest love or freedom to their fullest extent. It can also control the amount of God's Light it embraces through its own will; it can elevate itself to be a higher-dimensional existence, or reduce its amount of Light to downgrade itself to be a lower-dimensional existence.

In that case, is soul meant to have a nature that would permit it to commit evil, conceive vicious thoughts or be corrupt? Is it attributable to the creativity of soul that some people fall down to or create Hell? This question can be answered with both "Yes" and "No."

The affirmative answer is supported by the fact that the soul is given the freedom to create. That means that there can be no regulation of or obstacles in the way of the soul, or there is no freedom. On the other hand, the negative answer can be validated by the fact that soul was not originally created to commit evil or to create Hell. Evil does not lie dormant in soul itself. Evil is the manifestation of distortion and strain which develops out the conflicts between individuals while they exercise their freedom of that soul.

A man cannot commit any crime all by himself. Therefore, evil reveals itself only in the presence of other people, other life or other objects.

Since ancient times, there have been various arguments surrounding the dualism of vice and virtue. The fundamental questions have been, "Why does evil exist in the world created by God?" and, "Does evil lie dormant in God Himself?" However, evil does not represent a part of God's nature. Evil is nothing but the manifestation of distortion, for a specific period of time, in the phenomenal or spiritual world, as a result of the conflicts between individuals who are given freedom by God, or a conflict of freedoms between those individuals.

The second feature of soul is its function as the center of the concentration and radiation of God's Light.

What, then, is God's Light? It is God's energy which is omnipresent in the Macrocosm. Just as the Sun exists for the earth, does heat energy shower itself upon the high-dimensional and multi-dimensional universe beyond the third dimension. This heat energy is what is known as God's Light. Just as no creature on earth can survive without the Sun's heat energy, no life in the Real World can survive without God's Light or God's heat energy. The soul is endowed with a nature to concentrate, absorb, radiate and intensify God's Light. Those individuals who are capable of absorbing and radiating a massive amount of God's Light are considered to be people with a great amount of Light. They are called Guiding Spirits of Light. Those individuals who are referred to as Nyorais or Bosatsus have a tremendous capacity to concentrate and radiate God's Light as well as transfer it on to others. In other words, they can produce Light in the hearts of people.

All human souls live by absorbing and emitting God's

Light. However, High Divine Spirits like Nyorais and Bosatsus, who radiate God's Light in order to brighten up the world and fill people's hearts with Light as Guiding Spirits and Angels of Light, all have a device called "Powertron" shining on their chests. This device serves as proof that any individual who possesses it supplies God's Light to others but not to himself. Therefore, if one does not possess a Powertron on his chest when perceived through clairvoyance, he can not be regarded as a true Angel of Light even though he calls himself a great religious leader.

As mentioned above, the soul has the ability to concentrate and radiate God's Light. Is this also true with the evil spirits in the Hell Realm? The supply of God's Light energy to these spirits has certainly been exhausted. Actually, they themselves shield God's Light from entering their realm with the clouds of evil thoughts which they created.

They are living in dark and damp grotto-like places and no longer rely upon God's Energy to sustain their lives. Their source of energy is the evil thoughts that haunt the minds of the people on earth who absorb God's Light as spiritual energy and convert food into life energy, just like independent power generators. Evil spirits steal power from these generators by plug ging themselves into the cloudy, black parts of people's minds. They steal energy and vigor from people who then go insane. Hell spirits are, so to speak, vampires who absorb the energy of living humans.

To avoid being haunted by those Hell spirits, you

have to prevent them from plugging into your mind. You must not create, in your mind, a dark and damp place which will be compatible with Hell spirits, or cancerous cells which refuse God's Light. If everybody heeded these words, Hell would eventually disappear as evil spirits would be deprived of their energy supply.

3. The Personifications of God

I have explained in the previous section that Angels of Light are endowed with a device called Powertron on their chests. Now I would like to talk about Angels of Light.

An Angel sounds Christian, while a Bosatsu sounds very Buddhist. But an Archangel in Christianity equals a Nyorai in Buddhism, while Angels include the Buddhist Bosatsus and Shoten-Zenjins (Special Mission High Spirits).

As I have stated earlier, both Christianity and Buddhism trace their origins to God's teachings. The difference between them is the color of God's Light which was determined by the personality of their respective founders. So, it makes no difference whether you call High Divine Spirits, Angels of Light or Grand Guiding Spirits of Light. The point is that these high spirits appear to ordinary souls or common people as if they are the personifications of God.

The question is : why do high grade spirits, who can

be likened to personifications of God, exist? If God created humans to be equal, is it not already a form of discrimination for these high spirits to exist? Shouldn't an ordinary person lead an ordinary life while high spirits seek their own way?

The answer to this question is that God's view of the world consists of two principles: "equality" and "impartiality."

It is God's Truth that Buddha's nature inhabits all human beings, animals, plants and minerals. Regardless of the form in which it is presented as phenomenon, the fact that all things in the universe are expressions of God's Will is the indisputable Truth of God.

In other words, all living beings and all things in the universe consist of a diamond named God's Wisdom. To make a human exist as a human and a plant exist as a plant, God scatters diamonds in various ways and performs the beauty of creation. Every human being, every animal and every plant consists of God's diamond, named wisdom. This is the truth.

In Buddhism this diamond is referred to as Buddha's nature, which inhabits everything; while in Christianity, it is the origin of the notion that all human beings are children of God. Therefore, high spirits and low spirits are all equal in the sense that they represent God's Life. To think it unequal is to be misled by the words, "high" and "low."

The point is that there are highly evolved spirits, spirits on their way to evolve, and underdeveloped spirits. They all follow the same path. The difference is that some are ahead of others.

Highly evolved Guiding Spirits of Light walk ahead of others because they have longer histories as spirits. Generally, underdeveloped spirits have only short histories as spirits and are, therefore, walking behind. Can this fact be judged as unequal? Is it unequal to define the distance one has walked as simply that distance?

The fact must be evaluated from the viewpoint of impartiality rather than equality. Even though a spirit has a long history does not necessarily mean that it is well ahead of others because some go backwards. For instance, that this or that soul changed from an angel to a devil of Hell represents the case in which one began to reverse his direction after making respectable progress. Such spirits should be defined as regressed rather than underdeveloped spirits.

God strictly maintains equality because He allows every single spirit to follow the way leading towards Him. God also maintains fairness in the sense that every spirit is evaluated by the distance it advances towards God.

Therefore, high spirits who can be identified as personifications of God have shown significant progress and have been given special roles to play. All the other spirits are undertaking eternal training to reach the standard which is determined by the high spirits.

4. The Structure of the Spirit

I have explained that each human spirit or soul is in a different stage of development, which is governed from two viewpoints of God : "equality" and "impartiality." Next I would like to discuss the structure of soul.

It is said that the spirit consists of a "core" part and "branch" parts, or that human souls which appear on earth as superficial consciousnesses are only a part of the total consciousness, while the subconsciousness remains in the Real World.

In the beginning, the primordial God, which is regarded as an existence beyond the twentieth dimension, created a thirteen-dimensional consciousness, or the Cosmic Divine Spirit. In turn, the thirteen-dimensional consciousness created a twelve-dimensional nebular consciousness. This twelve-dimensional consciousness created an eleven-dimensional Star consciousness, and the eleven-dimensional consciousness created a ten-dimensional planetary consciousness. It is in the ninth dimension that personified consciousnesses can first be found. They are referred to as Divine Spirits or Divinity.

Even though a nine-dimensional Divine Spirit is a consciousness with a personality, the scale of its energy is too large for it to live in a human body. So only a part of its consciousness is used when a nine-dimensional Divine Spirit has to live in human flesh in the three-dimensional world. Moses and Jesus Christ are, for instance, personalized parts of the nine-dimensional Divine Spirits that dwelled in human bodies and were souls with personalities.

A soul is a spirit with the personality of a human being, and when it returns to the ninth dimension after leaving a human body, it is absorbed into the Grand Spirit to be a part of its memory field. From this viewpoint, a nine-dimensional Divine Spirit can divide itself into an infinite number of souls at will.

The situation is somewhat different for Grand Guiding Spirits of Light in the eighth dimension, Nyorai Realm. They are still Grand Spirits, but are more personalized and individualized. In general, a spirit in the eighth dimension lives in heaven as an integrated spirit and, when necessary, it can be divided into a number of entities. For instance, there exists the integrated eight-dimensional personality of Yakushi Nyorai (medicinal Nyorai), but the Light can be divided into thousands and tens of thousands of entities to give guidance to earthly or spiritual humans when help in the medical field is in high demand. Simply, even though an eight-dimensional Nyorai has an integrated personality, it can be split to facilitate the number of functions required of it. In this regard, it is different from the nine-dimensional Divine Spirit which can divide itself into different personalities for various purposes out of its own original quality of Light.

In the seven-dimensional Bosatsu Realm, a spirit's

personification is more advanced. While in the realms of the eighth and ninth dimensions there exist consciousnesses that have never appeared in the earthly world, seven-dimensional spirits, which principally form groups of six, have all experienced human life on the earth. Of the six, the leader is called a "core spirit" and the other five are called "branch spirits." These six alternately undertake activities on the earth as Bosatsus, guided by the spirit which is next in line for life on the ground as its guardian spirit. Each one's experience is shared in common and, therefore, the disposition of each soul is identical.

For example, St. Mark, a disciple of Jesus Christ and the author of the Gospel according to St. Mark, was reborn as St. Nichiro, a disciple of St. Nichiren in the Kamakura Period (1192 AD—1333 AD) in Japan. If you speak about Christianity to a consciousness of St. Nichiro, a consciousness as St. Mark can reply. Thus, a group of six souls forms a single spirit, just as five fingers and a palm form a hand.

Spirits in the six-dimensional Godly Realm are too individualized, and so have difficulty comprehending that six souls form a single spirit. It becomes more difficult to discuss with them, the concept of spiritual brothers or "core spirit" and "branch spirit."

Approximately one hundred million years ago, in the worlds including the Godly Realm and below, five branch spirits, or copies, were created from each six-dimensional spirit by intensifying and radiating God's Light with a gigantic device called "Pytron." Since the spiritual grades of these branch spirits were lower than those of the originals, these new spirits became inhabitants of either the five-dimensional Spiritual Realm or the four-dimensional Astral Realm. From the necessity to upgrade these human spirits, human beings were made to transmigrate between this and the other world for more than one hundred million years.

In the sixth dimension or below, the core spirit mainly guards or guides individual souls when they undertake trainings on the earth. When earthly experiences cause too great a spiritual discrepancy between the six souls—threatening their compatibility—a regrouping may take place.

5. The System of Guardian Spirits and Guiding Spirits

Religions often refer to a "guardian spirit" and a "guiding spirit." I would like to offer an explanation of these terms.

First, it is often said that an individual has his own guardian spirit, or that a powerful guardian spirit can improve your destiny, while a powerless one can bring you misfortune. The reality is that guardian spirits do exist and each individual is indeed allotted one. And it is true to some extent that a guardian spirit can influence one's life.

Next, I will reveal the secret of why guardian spirits

from the other world began to protect living humans.

Three hundred and some tens of millions of years ago, when humankind began living on earth, no human being was allotted a guardian spirit. As humans had pure hearts and minds, they could directly communicate with spirits in the Real World. Those people experienced daily, the so-called "spiritual path" phenomena. Every evening, everyone would sit cross-legged, meditate and reflect on the passed day while communicating with spirits in Heaven. Some people would leave their bodies during meditation in order to work in the Nyorai or Bosatsu Realm.

At that time, neither the Hell Realm nor devils existed. Both people on earth and in the Real World were always filled with good and harmonious thoughts. Consequently, there was no need to protect these people with guardian spirits.

However, about one hundred and twenty million years ago, spirits with disharmonious intentions began forming the dark Hell Realm within the fourth-dimensional Posthumous Realm, which is the lowest region of the other world. Moreover, God's light energy no longer shined in Hell, and so these evil spirits produced confusion in the earthly world, causing people to create negative energies, as an energy source for their survival. Hell spirits plotted to flood the world with disbelief and chaos by invading the minds of people on the ground and, therein, cause disharmony, war, anger, jealousy, complaints and other negative emotions. This development was completely unexpected.

In view of this situation, Grand Guiding Spirits of Light held an emergency conference in Heaven to work out counter measures. Led by Amor, or Jesus Christ as he is known today, they decided upon the following three measures :

1) People on earth shall not open their spiritual paths, in principle, to avoid being completely controlled by evil spirits, and shall strive to better their lives in the material world.

2) At birth, each individual shall be accompanied by a guardian spirit to protect him from temptations of the Hell Realm.

3) So that the Real World will not be totally forgotten, Grand Guiding Spirits of Light shall be sent to earth periodically, and shall preach religion to inform people of the Real World.

These three principles have been observed ever since, for more than one hundred million years. However, the Hell Realm has grown too large for a guardian spirit to protect a human being throughout his entire training on earth. Furthermore, ordinary people, other than religious leaders, who were restrained from opening a spiritual path, are unable to recall memories of past lives', and now indulge all the more in the materialism of the earthly world.

Moreover, the irony was that the establishment of religions on earth in regular intervals by Grand Guiding Spirits of Light caused struggles among religions and religious sects. Devils from Hell took advantage of these struggles and invaded the minds of religious leaders to distort their teachings. Thus, the earth became increasingly chaotic.

Against this background, it became necessary to improve the system of guardian spirits, not to mention the significance and urgency of our efforts to spread God's Truth.

As a general rule, the responsibility of being a guardian spirit is undertaken by one member of the group of six, consisting of a core spirit and branch spirits, who will next come down to the ground. However, in case the duty of someone on earth is so important that it must be completed quickly, it was decided that the person be accompanied by a guiding spirit who specialized in the subject which corresponds to the most important need of the person.

In the case of religious leaders, each one was accompanied by an Angel of Light whose spiritual grade was higher than his. Consequently, the system of guardian and guiding spirits became firmly established, although the destinies of people on earth are still being interfered with by various evil spirits.

6. The Evolution of Souls

Although earth has fallen into a disorderly state due to its connection with the Hell Realm in the last hundred million or so years, the terrestrial spirit group as a whole has not retrograded. Indeed, from a wide point of view, conspicuous progress can also be observed as a result of the evolution of souls.

Some of the souls who were created on earth achieved remarkable progress. Through their transmigrations, these superior souls steadily advanced from the fourth to the fifth, the fifth to the sixth, the sixth to the seventh dimensions and so on. Some earth-born souls have progressed to the point where they are equivalent to high spirits from other planets. To the delight of high dimensional Divine Spirits, some earthborn souls evolved to as high as the eight-dimensional Nyorai Realm, though not yet to the nine-dimensional Cosmic Realm.

This was the very result desired by the high spirits when they created the terrestrial spirit group. It also means that their dream came true ; when high grade spirits departed from their original stars, they hoped to make the earth more harmonized and more evolved than their own.

At present, the eight-dimensional Nyorai Realm has nearly five hundred Nyorais, and the seven-dimensional Bosatsu Realm has about nineteen thousand Bosatsus. Of these, one hundred and thirty Nyorai and seven thousand Bosatsus were born on earth. Also, a respectable number of Pytron-made souls progressed to be upper six-dimensional Shoten-Zenjins, or to seven-dimensional Bosatsus. This good news contrasts with the news of the expansion of the Hell Realm.

Then, why and how do souls evolve? I would like to address this question now.

First, to understand why souls evolve, we need to trace back to the origin of matter; why did God create souls of different grades? It is important to think about that before questioning why evolution is necessary.

If God's ultimate goal is to achieve a high degree of evolution with Himself standing at the apex, it is not necessary or logical to create low-grade souls for the process of evolution. I think that God created consciousnesses or souls of different grades and required them to evolve because He thought that perhaps much good would come as a result of the evolution process.

For example, if parents are completed forms, why do they need to give birth to and raise children? It is because their purpose is not to raise a child to be a perfect parent; they should find enjoyment in giving birth to and raising a child. Children make a home joyful and, therein, happiness develops.

The reason why God created consciousnesses or souls of various levels, the process of evolution and the development of these souls, is because He finds joy in the process of evolution itself. Through evolution, the creation of the Macrocosms and all life becomes an expression of God's joy and a source of His happiness.

That is the fundamental reason for the rules of the Macrocosmic evolution. God is watching the consciousnesses—or souls—he created evolve, develop and improve themselves towards Himself with infinite love.

Chapter II : God's Truth Speaks

Next, Let me explain how souls evolve.

One way to gage how far a soul has evolved is by the amount of Light it has. In the Real World, the amount of Light instantly shows the degree of individual soul growth. This is also applicable to the people on the ground. In accordance with one's advancement in the discipline of the soul towards enlightenment, one's amount of Light increases. As a result, a so-called aura begins to glow and one's level of enlightenment is easily perceived by someone with clairvoyance.

Any one whose mind is attuned to the Hell Realm has a dim aura, showing the parts whitened and irritated by being haunted by Hell spirits. One who is sympathetic to the four-dimensional Astral Realm has an aura of one or two centimeters set off of his whole body. Another, whose mind is attuned to the five-dimensional Spiritual Realm, has an aureola of three to four centimeters set off of the back of his head.

If one's mind becomes intimate with the six-dimensional Godly Realm, the aureola grows to be as much as ten centimeters off of his head. Angels of Light and Special Mission Spirits in the upper sixth dimension come to have a golden aureola shaped like a small tray. The seven-dimensional Bosatsu has a golden aureola of forty to fifty centimeters reaching his shoulders. And an eight-dimensional Nyorai radiates Light from one to two meters around him, brightening up his surroundings.

Thus, the extent that a soul has evolved can be expressed by an amount of Light. In other words, a

soul must enlarge its capacity to receive God's Light in
order to evolve. To do so, one must be rid of any
darkness in one's mind that may block God's Light.
Furthermore, one must devote oneself to the discipline
of the soul in order to enlarge its capacity.

7. The Relationship of Mind and Soul

In this section I would like to discuss the subject of
mind and soul.

I have already used the following words : consciousness, spirit and soul. Although the usage of these is not
strictly established, you may understand that the
attributes of a human being gradually develop from
consciousness, to spirit, to soul.

Then, is soul the same as mind? Let me explain this
subject.

The conclusion is that the mind is the core of the
soul. As the physical heart is positioned in the center
of a human body, the mind occupies the central part of
the soul, which corresponds to the physical body of a
spirit. The mind is not in the head, between cerebral
folds, nor inside brain cells.

The evidence is that when a human being dies and
returns to the other world, his memory of his lifetime is
not lost. When his flesh vanishes, his cerebral tissue
should naturally be lost—burnt and diffused as carbon
dioxide gas into the air. However, even if the cerebrum

is lost, the soul can think, feel and memorize. The brain is, so to speak, a filing cabinet with various information files, and an information control room. Therefore, if the brain, as a data-control room, gets damaged, a human being becomes unable to carry out logical judgment and action because the direction and ordering system of his body structure becomes disordered.

Let us suppose, for example, that someone is suffering from a mental disorder caused by brain damage. This person's family may think that nothing they say will make sense to him. The truth is, it will. In spite of his mental illness, he can understand what his family says to him. He understands everything through his mind or the core of his soul. He is violent, for example, only because he cannot express that he understands. For that reason, even if one should go insane or suffer from mental illness as a result of a physical defect, he will resume his thinking capabilities as a normal person when he returns to the other world after death.

If the mind is not in the brain, is it in the physical heart ? When a soul recognizes a mind, the physical heart certainly feels close to the mind, as far as its position is concerned. But the physical heart is meant to be an organ in charge of the blood circulation of a body and not the mind itself. On the other hand, it is also true that your heart beats quickly when your mind is disturbed, that your heart feels constricted with grief, and that your heart feels frozen with terror. When you are happy or sad, you may feel heat or tears coming up from somewhere near your heart.

All those facts should lead us to understand that the physical heart is closely related to the mind, and is an organ vulnerable to spiritual influence, even though the physical heart is not the mind itself. Therefore, if you imagine that the soul takes the shape of a human body, the mind is actually in the chest and governs mainly will, sentiment, instinct, reason and wisdom, and gives commands to the whole soul through another center that is positioned in the human brain. This center can be considered a branch of the mind.

Although a spirit is originally energy without shape, the spirit creates a soul in the shape of a human body, positions the "mind" at its center and undertakes trainings in life as a human being.

Many of you living on earth may flatly deny the existence of the spirit or soul, but you can't deny the existence of the "mind." Even someone with the materialistic view that the mind resides in the cerebral cortex cries quite naturally when he is sad, without pondering whether or not his situation warrants tears.

When you are sad, you feel a lump in your throat as tears pour forth from your eyes. When you unexpectedly come across an old friend, a strong feeling wells up inside and you cannot help hugging that person. These are not the functions of your cerebral cortex but your mind. I intend to discuss many aspects of this mystery of mind.

8. The Function of Mind

A human being is a consciousness, a spirit and a soul created by the will of God. I have stated this repeatedly. I have also explained that the core, or the center of the soul is the mind.

Now, I would like to investigate the mind further. The actions and functions of the mind are what we will be exploring.

It is often said that one's "thought" gets across to others. It actually happens that if you like someone, this "thought" is communicated to that person and he or she, in turn, begins to like you. On the contrary, if you dislike a person in your mind, the very "thought" gets across to the person and he or she becomes cold. Why does this telepathy actually occur? Let us consider this question.

The "function of mind" is the creativity which God granted to humankind. God created each dimensional structure with an initial "idea" as its origin. So created, also, is the three-dimensional universe, human souls and even human flesh. A human is a part of God's consciousness and at the same time represents a complete microcosm. Therefore, the function of the human mind is derived from the same root as the "creative function" of God. Every single thought and imagination is creating something in this three-dimensional

65

space and somewhere in the multi-dimensional universe. The mass of "ideas" by individuals includes the power to form and perpetuate the Real World.

There is more than one kind of "thought," and each "thought" differs in its stage or level.

First, "thinking" is a kind of thought that pops up in one's mind on various occasions in everyday life and can be regarded as a part of the regular intellectual activities of individuals.

Next, "imagination" is more substantial. If "thinking" can be likened to waves that constantly erode a seashore, "imagination" is a vision which is more continuous and substantial; it can be visualized and expressed as an image. It has continuity and direction like the waters of a flowing river.

Moreover, we come to the stage of thought known as "will." Thought at this stage is distinctly creative. It even has a sort of physical power, psychokinesis. In the multi-dimensional universe starting from the fourth dimension, the "will" creates various things by means of a creativity similar to that of God. Also, in the third dimension, "will" is a mental force with considerable physical power.

For example, when the "will" that guides people in a positive direction is concentrated on one individual, this person's state of mind changes drastically or his environment suddenly improves. On the contrary, when a hateful "will" is concentrated on someone, that person may fall ill, have bad luck or even die.

The previous example is applicable to a mass of

people as well. If hundreds of thousands, or millions of people want to make this world a kingdom of God, or Utopia, and that "will" becomes concentrated and magnified, a Light will shine forth from one corner of the earth. The Light will then go into people's minds and they will create a world of happiness. As a result, this Earthly Realm will change into the "Bosatsu Realm."

Of course, the complete opposite can happen. Imagine that this world became filled with evil-will such as hate, anger and selfishness. From a spiritual point of view, it would appear as if black thoughts like thunderclouds hovered above various parts of the earth, and that these thoughts would turn into a physical energy to unleash confusion on the earth.

Thus, the function of the human mind is wonderful and at the same time dreadful. Therefore, we must reflect upon ourselves and check the behavior of our minds.

9. One Thought Leads to Three Thousand Worlds

Now that I have talked about the gradually intensifying power of thought, thinking, imagination and will, let me advance my explanation of the concept, "one thought leads to three thousand worlds."

It was a Chinese priest, the Grand Master T'ien-t'ai Chih-i (Tendai Chigi in Japanese), who once preached this concept one thousand and several hundreds of years ago on Mt. T'ien-t'ai in China, and I was the very person who gave him guidance from heaven during his lifetime. The following is a summary of what I communicated to him :

"The human mind has an indicator of thought. The indicator constantly points in different directions and never stops. Even a person who was confirmed in Buddhism and undergoing severe discipline sometimes has his indicator of thought swayed by a beautiful young female or appetizing food. His indicator of thought, or his mind, moves when he sees others attaining enlightenment ahead of him. While being scolded by his mentor, the indicator may waver again. Thus, his mind is never at peace."

"True enlightenment for a human is found only in great harmony and calmness, never in such an unstable mind. T'ien-t'ai Chih-i, you must understand this deeply, and clearly show people the proper direction in which their indicators of thought should point, otherwise, people can never obtain a true peace of mind. As a compass never fails to indicate North, the indicator of people's minds should point to Divinity. As the Polaris always directs people to the North, T'ien-t'ai Chih-i, you must enlighten people and lead them to follow the will of Divinity. Such is the true, unshakable mind and true faith."

"The mind is truly mysterious. If one's mind is like that of the Ashura (Asura in Sanskrit) demon, he will sympathize with the Ashura Hell, and eventually be led to live a life full of fighting and destruction."

"When the indicator of one's mind is fixed towards lust, the mind is connected with the Lust Hell and demons will step into the living human's mind by climbing up the fixed indicator. As a result, the person loses perspective on women or men and ends up as a vehicle through which demons satisfy their lust."

"When the direction of a religious person's mind becomes distorted or extremely self-sufficient and self-congratulatory, he may preach distorted, evil teachings led by the voice of devils mistaken for the voice of Nyorai or Bosatsu. The poor religious leader will eventually fall down to Infinite Hell himself, as a result of misguiding people."

"Or, there is a person who is of good will and sympathizes with the Heavenly Realm of good people (five-dimensional Spiritual Realm), and always receives blessings from his ancestors and friends in Heaven. Another kind of person never ceases to care for other people, is always modest, unassuming and seeking the way to God. His mind sympathizes with the Bosatsu Realm, as he is actually living a Bosatsu's life."

"Another person directs the indicator of his mind only towards diffusing the Right Laws or God's Truth. He teaches correctly, has a noble personality and is living a truly respectable life. His mind is attuned to the Nyorai Realm while living on the ground, and various Nyorais in Heaven guide him always."

"The indicator of mind functions in such mysterious

ways. T'ien-t'ai Chih-i, you have to understand this Truth fully and help living people in their disciplines."

"Heaven and Hell don't only exist after death. Both of them exist in this world, right in the minds of people. The indicator of mind can instantly indicate Heaven or Hell in the other world. This is what I mean by 'one thought leads to three thousand worlds'. If people get to know this truth, they will hold their thoughts for a short while every day, calm their minds, reflect on their lives, their day and then correct their minds and behavior accordingly."

"T'ien-t'ai Chih-i, the Eightfold Path was based on this very concept of 'one thought leads to three thousand worlds'. Because Heaven and Hell exist in living people's minds, not only after their death, and people's behavior defines their lives in the next world. Therefore, people must follow the Eightfold Path as the standard of life."

"The Eightfold Path refers to Right View, Right Thought, Right Speech, Right Work, Right Living, Right Effort, Right Will and Right Concentration of Mind. Upon mastering the Eightfold Path, one can maintain his mind in the right state, and accomplish his task as a human being."

"T'ien-t'ai Chih-i, preach the true concept of 'one thought leads to three thousand worlds'. Correct your thoughts and behavior based upon this Eightfold Path and this shall be your enlightenment and enlightenment for the people of the world."

10. The Genuine Eightfold Path

To conclude this chapter, I would like to explain the significance of the Eightfold Path in the current age.

Human beings are blind. They search for a way to live in ignorance of the world beyond the information provided by their five senses. The true significance of life, however, exists beyond the five senses of the human race though, paradoxically, the clue to know the world beyond lies within the five senses. Therefore, we must sharpen our five senses, however blind we are, and strive to reach the Truth ; we mustn't only complain about our blindness. The Eightfold Path will manifest itself in the course of our efforts to seek God's Truth.

The Eightfold Path is the route to fulfillment as a human being. It is the wisdom to correct the direction of rightness.

There is no model to show how one should live his life because life consists of a series of questions asked in completely different ways, depending upon the individual's background, experience, knowledge and habits. No one but you can answer your own questions. It is you who may be off the right path. Who but you can reorient yourself ?

Therefore, each one of us must honestly seek "Rightness" within the frame of our lives.

71

The Laws of the Sun

Now, what is the guideline for that "Rightness"?
What defines "Rightness"? It is the vocation of genuine religious leaders. Indeed, the vocation of my
current life is to answer this question.

To know "Rightness" is to know God's Mind. It is
to study God's Life. What is right and what is wrong ;
what is genuine and what is false ; what is beautiful
and what is ugly. It is God's Mind which gives answers
to these questions. To know God's Mind is to research
the quality of God's Light energy. It means to make
thorough efforts to understand Him.

To let you understand God's Mind or the properties
of God as energy, I am introducing the words of High
Spirits by publishing my communications with them.
Spiritual communications from High Spirits should be
the most important clue to know God's Mind. Therefore, I wish you to comprehend God's Mind, and to
grasp "rightness" through High Spirits' words so that
you may have the correct direction for your own
Eightfold Path.

The criterion through which to evaluate the genuineness of the words of High Spirits which I have been
communicating to you is whether or not you have been
moved and impressed by them. If you cannot find
anything that truly touches your soul in these books,
you can abandon them and seek your own way for
"rightness" based on your own standards. However, if
you can believe in the words of High Spirits as representatives of God, you should follow their teachings as
the guidelines of your life. It is eventually your true self

which decides "rightness." The question is whether or not the divinity deep inside you agrees and sympathizes with this message.

I wish for you to lead your daily life with reference to the divinity in yourself, to comprehend and sympathize with it, and the following check points as the base of your reflections :

1) Did I see things and people rightly. Did I treat people with a Godlike heart ?

2) Did I speak rightly. Didn't I say things against my conscience ? Didn't I say what may lead others into confusion and anxiety ? Didn't I hurt others with my words ?

3) Did I think rightly. Didn't I conceive evil thoughts ? As evil thoughts pollute the world, I must keep my heart pure.

4) Did I work rightly. Did I effectively use the time granted by God, which is as precious as a diamond ? Did I use the time for the benefit of people ?

5) Did I live rightly. Didn't I have complaints ? Did I learn how to be content ? Was I thankful for all things ?

6) Am I studying God's Truth rightly ? Am I not loosing respect for Divinity ? How many people's minds did I save ?

7) Do I have the right plan for my life ? Do my prayers for self-actualization agree with God's Mind and serve to ennoble my own character ?

8) Do I have sufficient time for right concentration ? Did I reflect upon my past sin, my past day, and thank

my guardian and guiding spirits before going to sleep ?

The Genuine Eightfold Path—the eight points that indicate the right way for a human being to live—still maintains its value in the present age. To correct your daily life in this way will lead you to a remarkable life and eventually elevate you to the heights of Divinity.

Chapter III
The Great River of Love
•

The Great River of Love

•

1. What is Love ?

Together with the reader, I would like to consider the subject of love in this chapter. As love is my greatest concern, perhaps it is also the most important matter for the reader.

In the course of life as a human being, love is the most valuable and wonderful thing we encounter. We are enchanted by the sound of the word "love." The word "love" contains dreams, passion and romance.

Suppose today were the last day you had to live on this earth. Even if you were to die tonight, you would depart for death with a smile on your face if someone whispered words of love in your ear.

A life without love can be likened to that of a weary traveler who is walking in a desert. On the other hand, a life with love is similar to that of a traveler who occasionally sees oases and blooming flowers along the way.

What is love ? Who can clearly define love ? A man of letters ? Perhaps a poet ? Maybe a philosopher ? Or a man of religion ? The extent to which we can grasp the meaning and essence of love is a theme and a question imposed upon us by God. The pursuit of love brings joy and happiness, but also causes suffering and pain.

Love contains two extremes : the greatest of happiness and the greatest of misery. Although love can be a major source of joy in one's life, it can also be a major cause of suffering. It seems as if a streak of light is shining from the direction in which we look to grasp the essence of love, in order that we may control love and attain happiness. In the same way, it also seems that God is waiting for us with a big smile and outspread arms.

At any rate, in this chapter I will consider the essence of love, the different stages of love, love and enlightenment, and God and love.

I often discuss the subject of love with my Guiding Spirit, Jesus Christ. Christ is, of course, a master of love, an expert in love and a personification of God's love. Christ says, "Modern people are the very ones to whom we must relay the true meaning of love." According to Christ, there have been very few periods in recorded history in which love was as misunderstood as in modern times. These were the late days of Atlantis and the age of Sodom and Gomorrah in the Old Testament.

In any case, I would like to seriously ponder the

subject of love and to answer contemporary people's questions concerning the matter.

The search for love along the Eightfold Path is certainly the ideal way to cultivate our souls in life. That is the gospel of the modern age. Therefore, I would like to talk much about love. The discussion will be a view of life, a view of the world and God's Truth as these are seen from the fixed standpoint of love.

2. The Existence of Love

Although we have many opportunities to think about love, no one has seen it. It is impossible to hold onto love, see it or show it to others.

However, there is no doubt that love exists and I believe in the existence of love.

Man begins his endless journey, without a destination, in quest for the existence of love—something tangible that everyone can recognize as love.

No one who has actually seen love with his own eyes, and no one who has touched it with his own hands. Can it be that love is merely an illusion or a mirage?

Stop to think, however, how strongly human beings believe in the existence of things that can never be seen or touched. Take the wind, for example. We are unable to see the wind with our eyes. Nevertheless, we believe that it exists when we see a bunch of leaves whirling through the air or rustling in the trees. We are familiar with the tenderness, coldness and the vigor of the wind because it touches our skin. We can express what the wind is, but cannot capture wind, store it in a box or take it out to show to others.

Love is like the wind. Everybody believes in its existence and shares the feeling that it exists, but no one can prove its existence objectively. We cannot prove the existence of love. We cannot touch or look at love, but we can, indeed, feel its existence.

Love is very similar to God! Many people have talked about and believed in God, but not one of them has been able to touch Him or show Him to others. Many great minds have spoken about God, religion, philosophy, poetry and literature, but no one has been able to prove God's existence.

Even Jesus Christ could not show the image of God to people. He could not say to others, "Look at this Man, He is our Heavenly Father." Jesus used to say, "People who listen to my words listen to the words of my Father in Heaven since my Father is here speaking these words with me. People who see what I do, see the deeds of my Father in Heaven since He is making me do them." In other words, Jesus was constantly teaching people to feel God through what he said and did. Therefore, people were able to feel the presence of God through his authoritative words, and thus embrace Him.

Although there are many things of the utmost importance to people, the existence of these things cannot be proved. This has always been the case, regardless of the age. It is usually impossible to prove the existence of the most important things.

God, love, courage, wisdom, goodness, kindness, beauty, harmony, progress, mercy, truth, sincerity and altruism : these concepts are omnipresent existences in the universe, and there is no one in the World of Light who is unaware of them. However, nobody on this earth can firmly prove the existence of these things. All of these important things exist in the Real World beyond the third dimension and, therefore, it is impossible to prove their existence through three-dimensional methods.

God, as I now perceive Him, is the ultra-high dimensional being over twenty dimensions. It is, therefore, impossible to prove His existence through three-dimensional criteria. That is why there is something we call "faith." The Japanese word for "faith" consists of two Chinese characters which mean "believe" and "look up." To believe is to perceive and accept. To look up is to respect a great presence and humble oneself.

Jesus said, "God is love." It is true that love is surely one of God's attributes, but what Jesus really meant was more than that :

"The existence of God cannot be proved. If I dare to mention something akin to God, it is love. Isn't the existence of love impossible to prove ? Doesn't everybody know the glory of love, even if no one can prove its existence ? Doesn't everybody try to be loved and believe in the power of love ?

"Faith is another such thing. Those who believe in love should believe in God. Those who believe in the power of love should believe in the power of God because God is love. I, Jesus Christ, who am the son of God, perform acts of love. These acts are performed not by me, but by my Father in heaven, my God. He is here with me and makes me do them. If you want to see love, look at what I do. You will find love and God there."

The above is a restored version of the story of love that Jesus Christ spoke at Nazareth some two thousand years ago. I know these words well because it was I who guided Jesus from the Heavenly World, just as Jesus is now guiding me.

3. The Power of Love

As far as I know, love is the strongest power on earth. In fact, love is the strongest power in the multi-dimensional worlds beyond the third dimension. Furthermore, the power of love increases as the dimension of the realm increases because the power of love is the power of unity. The force of mutual rejection weakens people. However, unity doubles or triples a person's original power. Love, therefore, has no enemies. Nothing can stand in the way of love.

Love is a combat tank that climbs up hills, descends into valleys, crosses rivers, goes through swamps, forever shattering the fortresses of evil.

Love is light. It illuminates the darkness of night, the past, the present and the future. It illuminates Heaven, earth and the hearts of people. It even envelops the evils and sorrow of this world with infinite tenderness and warmth.

Love is life. For all people, love is the food, the power and the flame of life because love is all. Without love, there would be no life, death, way or hope. Love is anything and everything, the food of life and life itself.

Love is a disease. Once afflicted with it, everyone suffers from passion and cannot sleep. Within this very passion, however, there exists truth and the ever-lasting vigor of life.

Love is courage. Without love, man cannot be inspired ; without love, man cannot face up to death. Love is a torch with which to light a detonating fuse leading to God's Truth, and an arrow shot at delusions.

Love is a pledge. People live together, talk together and walk together in the name of love. Without the bond called love, people would be at a loss and have nothing to do but wait in vain for the twilight of life.

Love is words. Without words, there is no love ; without love, there are no words. Love is a good word, good thought, good vibration and good melody. God creates worlds with words, and love creates humankind through words.

Love is harmony. Only through love can people love each other, forgive each other, help each other and create a splendid world. Within the realm of love, there is no anger, jealousy or envy. Within this splendid realm only great harmony exists and everybody lives in peace.

Love is joy. Without love there can be no true joy or true happiness. Love is God's expression of joy; it is the magic that wipes out sorrow in this world. Love is joy, joy creates love and that love, in turn, creates joy. Thus, love is a circle or circulation.

Love is progress. One love creates one progress and one Light. Days with love are days with progress because God and innumerable Divine Spirits stand on the way to love. There is no regression or fear where there is love, only progress and improvement. Love is simply to fly toward the place of God.

Love is eternal. Love exists in the past, in the present and in the future. Never has there been a time or an age which has seen people without love. Love is a brilliant golden wing that flies through all ages. It is a Pegasus that runs through heaven far above. Love is the proof that life is eternal, and is a hunter which captures the present moments of infinite time.

And finally, love is prayer. Without love there is no prayer, and without prayer there is no love. The power of love is made more positive through prayer; love accomplishes everything through prayer. Prayer is the power by which love may be strengthened, and the secret method by which love may be deepened. Love succeeds and is fulfilled through prayer to God.

God is love; love is God. And prayer is what makes

love God. People live and know God by prayer. Thus, humans can maximize the power of love by prayer.

4. The Mystery of Love

Love is truly mysterious. It has infinite depth and infinite height. The more one thinks about love the more enriching it becomes.

Hesitant to show Himself before men, God most likely sent love to earth as a substitute. I believe that God has given humankind the materials through which to understand His true nature by allowing humans to learn about love.

The mystery of love—love makes us feel the existence of an invisible force. That is why love is mysterious. Let me introduce an allegory on the mystery of love.

Once upon a time there lived an old man. This old man lived a lonely life without children or grandchildren. He dwelled in a temple at the far corner of a village where children came to play from time to time. Taro was the naughtiest of all the boys. He was thirteen years old and, having lost his parents when he was just an infant, was raised by his sister and her husband.

One day, as Taro was playing on the stone steps that led to the temple, three sparrows came. They landed very close to where Taro was sitting and began to speak.

The Laws of the Sun

The first sparrow said, "The most wonderful thing in this world is the sun. We are able to enjoy the various colors in the world because the sun is shining in the sky. The trees and flowers are similarly overjoyed. Also because of the sun, grains grow in abundance even to spare for us sparrows."

"If the sun were to disappear, this world would become dark and no living creature could survive. Since we sparrows are always so thankful to the sun we never kill one another. Human beings, however, foolishly feel elated and have everything their own way because the sun is always smiling and shining down upon them. They fight and speak ill of one another. Some fools even fight wars. So, the time may come when the sun disappears, being fed up with the deeds of human beings."

After listening to this story the second sparrow said : "In my opinion, the most splendid thing in the world is water. Without water no living creature in the world could survive. The trees and grass would wither in one week if water disappeared. Without water, wheat and rice could not grow and we would die. Animals cannot live even one week without water. So our lives depend upon water, and I think that water is the most wonderful thing in the world."

"Since we sparrows are so thankful for water we are able to live happily together. But foolish human beings think little of water, and they are perfectly willing to work and sweat in order to obtain useless things such as jewels and necklaces. We sparrows are satisfied to appear as God made us, but human beings are always trying to find a way to look better. It is quite absurd that they should try to become superior to others, earn more money than others or become more beautiful than others."

Next, the third sparrow broke his silence and said :

"Surely, as both of you say, the sun and water are wonderful things. But the most valuable thing in the world is something that everybody takes for granted. No one notices the real value of its existence. I think the most valuable thing is the air. Even if the sun and water were to disappear, we would still be able to live for a few days. But if the air should suddenly disappear we could not live for more than one minute. Although you may recognize the importance of air now that I have pointed it out to you, air is really hard to appreciate."

"We sparrows inhale air into our chests and are thankful for the air when we fly in the sky. When the fish in the water suffer from a lack of oxygen, they also come up to the surface of the water, gasp, inhale the air and are thankful for it. In comparison to this, how arrogant human beings are ! They think that it is their intelligence that makes it possible for them to fly in their airplanes. That is not so. An airplane can fly because there is air. The air does not demand any money when we fly or when airplanes fly in the sky. We thank the air, but have never seen human beings doing so."

Taro became very sad after listening to the three

sparrows and became absorbed in thought. "I was taught that man was the lord of all creation and have never heard a story like the ones the sparrows have told. I have never before considered the precious value of the sun, water or the air. What a foolish creature man is! He is inferior even to the sparrows!"

After thinking such thoughts, Taro dashed up the stone steps. Startled by his sudden movement, the three sparrows flew away and disappeared. Taro visited the old man in the temple and told him the stories that he had just heard from the three sparrows. Taro cried to the man, saying that he wished he had been born a sparrow instead of a human, if human beings were so stupid. The old man replied:

"Taro, my boy, I am proud of you, for you have understood well. Human beings are foolish creatures who have lost sight of the most valuable things. Even these creatures, however, are forgiven through the act of loving each other. Human beings are ugly. But ugliness will not disappear no matter how much you gaze on that ugliness."

"God has given human beings a magical power called love to forgive their sins and erase the ugliness of humankind. And because of the mysterious power of love, man is permitted to be the lord of all creatures."

5. Love Has No Enemies

Love, the strongest of all powers, has no enemies. Here, I would like to discuss why love has no enemies.

The human being encounters various difficulties in the course of his life through which he can train his soul. It is programmed in advance. Exactly what are these difficulties ? They may include sickness, poverty, a setback, a hapless love affair, failure in business, separation from a friend, separation from your loved one, and encounters with those you hate. The human being inevitably gets old, he becomes ugly and disabled, and dies.

If these phenomena are taken simply as they are, then human life may be regarded as being full of suffering and sorrow. But suffering and sorrow have their own meanings. They compel us to choose. And what is the choice ? It is the choice between a life of giving and a life of receiving.

The essence of love is to give. Love means to share with others what you have received from God, rather than keeping it for yourself. God's Love is infinite. Therefore, no matter how we share it with others, it can never be exhausted. God constantly supplies love to us.

The essence of love is to give first. I hope you understand this point very well.

Those who suffer in love, please listen carefully. Why are you distressed ? Why do you fret about love ? Is it because you give love to others ? Do you not ask for rewards ? Asking for reward is not true love. True love is the "love that gives." It is a love without return. The love that you give does not originally belong to yourself. Your love was granted by God. In order to return this love to God, you must love others.

You suffer when you think that you love others, but they do not love you. However, it is not true that others do not love you. Love leads a human being to suffer when he thinks that others do not love him as much as he expects them to. Love's reward does not come from other people, but from God.

What, then, is this reward which comes from God ? It is that the more love you give, the more godlike you will become. This is the reward given by God.

Look at the essence of God. God gives infinite love and mercy to all creation without any reward, just like the sun which radiates brilliant rays of light. Is it not true that even your individual lives are the energy granted by God, without expectation of anything in return ? If so, start giving. To give means to live everyday with consideration of how as many people as possible can live happily. It also means to bestow the light of love upon as many lost people as possible. And furthermore, giving means to help as many people as possible regain the strength they have lost through difficulties and failures, and to help them spend their days wisely and courageously.

Give with your wisdom. Giving material things is not what giving is all about. Nor is being overly generous to charities.

The true act of giving is the way to let others live truly, and in order to let others live truly, the act of love should be accompanied by wisdom. Therefore, with wisdom and courage, let us lead lives of a giving nature or lives that give love to others without return.

Love has no enemies. Love is invincible. True love is the love that gives, which requires no return, and which is the irresistible and infinite power. Love is a large river that infinitely flows downstream.

No one can go against the current of this large river because love is the power to give everything, to wash away everything. No evil in this world can eternally resist love.

6. The Theory of Staged Development of Love

I have just finished discussing various aspects of love. I have said that true love is one that gives without any desire for reward. Based upon this, I must now tell the truth of how love has different stages of development.

Yes, there are stages in the development of love. Not many people on this earth, however, seem to have noticed this truth.

The first stage in the development of love is a "love

that loves." In a sense, this "love that loves" characterizes love most appropriately. It includes parental love toward one's child, filial love toward one's parents, a man's love toward a woman, a woman's love toward a man and love toward a friend or neighbor. In a broader sense, the "love that loves" includes love toward society and the community.

The "love that loves" can be regarded as one form of the "love that gives" because it is based on love toward an object for which one has a natural concern. To bestow goodwill upon an object with which one is naturally concerned is the meaning of the "love that loves." Although this is the most fundamental and common form of love, it is actually quite difficult to achieve.

This world would become a paradise if the earthly world were filled with this "love that loves." The "love that loves" can be expected from everyone, as everyone has the innate ability to understand the glory of this love. By their very nature, human beings feel happiness in giving love. The problem, however, does not always lie in understanding the "love that loves," but rather in practicing it. If the "love that loves" is truly brought into practice, the earthly world would be transformed into the equivalent of the five-dimensional Spiritual Realm (the realm of the good) while still in the third dimension. Thus, the realization of this "love that loves" is the initial step towards earthly Heaven.

The second stage in the development of love is a "love that nurtures." While the "love that loves" can be achieved by everyone, though it is difficult to practice, the "love that nurtures" cannot be realized by everyone. One who can nurture others is someone who is superior ; however, unless a person has firmly displayed that he is good enough to lead, by his talents and efforts, he can never nurture others. In other words, a "love that nurtures" is a "love that leads." In order to practice this love, one must first build an excellent character in himself because the blind cannot lead the blind.

Like the water of a river which flows downstream, this "love that nurtures" flows from high to low. The "love that nurtures" is a love of intelligence and reason. Therefore, unless one has the intelligence to grasp the true nature of humankind and society, and the profound reason with which to solve the problems of these, he cannot truly lead other people. He wouldn't be able to truly nurture other people.

In this sense, the "love that nurtures" can be regarded as the love of the six-dimensional "Godly Realm" in the Real World. There are some earthly leaders, of course, who can practice the "love that nurtures"; their minds are actually attuned to the six-dimensional "Godly Realm" in Heaven while still living on the ground.

The "love that loves" bestows goodwill upon those for whom the person has a natural concern. The "love that nurtures" enables the person to lead others by building an excellent character in himself. Both of these are splendid forms of love. However, the "love that nurtures" is not in itself sufficient because if the only necessary form of love is that which nurtures others, it could be realized by anyone with superior talent or superior intelligence. There is a love which goes beyond talent, intelligence and effort. It is the third stage of love, the "love that forgives."

In order to practice the "love that forgives," one must experience a great leap towards a spiritual state of mind. This love belongs to the state of mind in which one can "love thy enemy." This state can only be realized by one who is extremely broad-minded and tolerant of others, and whose virtue goes beyond mere ability.

Only one who can regard all human beings as the children and the very selves of God can love and forgive those who appear to be his enemy. In other words, the state of mind that is capable of the "love that forgives" is that of Bosatsu. Therefore, one who practices this "love that forgives" is an envoy from the seventh dimension, and his mind is attuned to the Bosatsu Realm of the Real World.

Even in this "love that forgives," however, there remains the inclination of mind that regards evil as evil and an enemy as an enemy. This kind of love is still not free from the dualism of vice and virtue, and is far from the state of God's Mind in which even evil and enemies are forgiven. True love should surpass the dualism of vice and virtue. If one forgives his enemies as enemies, and if he regards himself as being superior to others, seats himself on the throne and thus forgives

others, he has not truly attained spiritual enlightenment.

Here lies the difference between the mind of Bosatsu
and that of Nyorai. A Bosatsu is still not free from the
dualism of vice and virtue, and so struggles to expel evil
and grasp goodness. Next, I would like to discuss the
stage of love that goes beyond this.

7. The Love as Existence and the Love of God

What, then, is this higher state of love that exceeds
the "love that forgives"? It is no longer a love between
one and another. I would name it, "love as existence."
It exceeds even the relationship between the superior
and the inferior.

"Love as existence" can be realized when the mere
existence of some one with whom we have experienced
only one brief encounter shatters our illusions, brings
about spiritual enlightenment and a turning point in
our lives, leading us to convert from evil to good. This
is the love of a person who, simply by living on this
earth during a particular age, brightens the world and
lights the torch of hope for humankind. His mere act
of loving someone and his speaking of beautiful words
or bestowing of kindness upon others is not necessarily
considered love. Rather, his existence itself is love, and
his character is the very existence of love. We may call
such a person the personification of "love as exis-

tence." Surely this kind of person has a brilliant place in the history of humankind.

If "love that forgives" can be likened to the love of a virtuous man of religion, then "love as existence" can be likened to the love of a great mind that stands out in the history of humankind. Such love can be likened to the light of this world, and the spirit of age.

I have mentioned that "love as existence" is not a one-to-one love.

That is to say that it is a one-to-many form of love, or a love which is emitted like radiation. It is existence as Light, or a personification of Light.

The above should lead you to understand what state of mind represents this stage of love. Yes, it is the love of the eight-dimensional Nyorai Realm. Accordingly, one who realizes "love as existence" in a particular age is a Nyorai, and his very incarnation in this world is mercy for humankind. Mercy is the light of love that impartially illuminates everything; it is not a relative love that varies in amount depending upon the object of one's love. In other words, mercy is an "absolute love," and a "love of fairness."

Love develops beginning with the five-dimensional "love that loves," then goes on to the six-dimensional "love that nurtures." This development continues to the seven-dimensional "love that forgives," and is followed by "love as existence" at the eight-dimensional stage. Being familiar with these stages of love is sufficient for the purpose of training in life.

There is, of course, also a four-dimensional love,

which is the "love of instinct." The way in which one uses his instincts determines whether he is attuned to the Hell Realm or the Astral Realm. But this is not the love for which the trainee should aim.

The highest stage of love for humankind on the earth is nine-dimensional love. This is "love as a personification of God" and the "love of the Messiah." I do not insist that people aim at this love as their soul training because this stage of love is for one who has been chosen as the tool of God, or the best proxy of God. If an unqualified religious leader should try to preach the "love of the Messiah," the next world awaiting him will be the deepest part of the four-dimensional Hell Realm, known as "Infinite Hell." It is because in the Real World, incorrectly conveying God's message is the most vicious crime—much worse than robbery or murder. It is considered to be a heinous crime because such preaching spoils the eternal soul, which is more precious than human life on earth.

Therefore, we must be satisfied with the simple knowledge that the "love of God," a great love that leads humankind and wishes progress on humankind, exists beyond "love as existence."

And so, the development of love begins with the "love of instinct," a love which requires no special effort. This progresses to the "love that loves," then the "love that nurtures," on to the "love that forgives" and next to "love as existence." To attain these stages of love should be our objective. Then, in the last stage there is the "love of God," which is beyond the scope of the human mind.

8. Love and the Genuine Eightfold Path

In chapter II, I explained the true meaning of the Eightfold Path. And in this chapter, I have introduced the theory of "staged development of love." Now, I would like to talk about the relationship between these two teachings.

In the discussion on the Eightfold Path, I mentioned that there were eight steps for man to live a right life. I said that these steps were the guidelines for daily enlightenment and the way to attain enlightenment. On the other hand, in the theory of "Staged Development of Love," I said that there were four stages as objectives in our training : the "love that loves, love that nurtures, love that forgives and love as existence" (See the Table of Dimensional Structures on page 217).

Comparing these two teachings, we find that the Eightfold Path emphasizes daily training and daily enlightenment. On the other hand, the theory of "staged development of love" is targeted at more or less a medium-range or long-range purpose, while starting with daily life.

With regard to the relationship of these two ways to spiritual enlightenment, I dare to suggest the following :

1) Right View and Right Speech correspond to the

stage of the "love that loves."

2) Right Work and Right Living correspond to the stage of the "love that nurtures."

3) Right Thought and Right Effort in searching for the way, correspond to the stage of the "love that forgives."

4) Right Will and Right Concentration of mind correspond to the stage of "love as existence."

Now I would like to expand on each of the above.

First, Let's discuss why Right View and Right Speech correspond to the stage of the "love that loves." The "love that loves" is a love toward someone with whom one is naturally concerned. To be friendly toward the object of his love, one must first see the object in a right way : "What does he need now ? What is he worried about ?" It is necessary to notice such matters. Once one has achieved the Right View, the next step is to speak rightly. One must offer helpful advice or warm words to encourage him, or appropriate comments to help him recover from his difficulties.

Right Work and Right Living are included in the stage of the "love that nurtures." What does Right Work, or working in a right way mean ? All human beings are meant to work in order to live ; to obtain food, a human being must work. Therefore, to work in a right way means to accomplish something that is helpful to other people, and to fulfill one's mission as a child of God.

Right Living means to fulfill one's own life or to live in the right way. Human beings cannot live in solitude as it is impossible to live completely alone. We live in a community consisting of various people who cooperate with each other and, thus, enlighten each other. In other words, a right life offers an opportunity to nurture each other and, therefore, practice the "love that nurtures." Thus, Right Work and Right Living are positioned at the stage of the "love that nurtures."

Third, Right Thought and Right Effort in searching for the way are included in the stage of the "love that forgives." Right Thought or thinking in a right way, means the ability to adjust human relations by seeing them with true eyes. One must not be misled by the appearance of others as physical human beings. Rather, one should see his true self as an inhabitant of the Real World, and foster the right relationship with that person. We should think about each other's ideal state as children of God. There must not be any enemy or unforgivable villains. If we achieve Right Thought, our minds are always generous, and so permit us to embrace everything. At this point, our state of mind will naturally elevate to the stage of the "love that forgives."

The same could be said for Right Effort. Right Effort in searching for the way means to make every effort to grasp God's Truth, and to deepen one's enlightenment day by day. If one searches for the way toward Divinity in a right way, there will be no anger, no grumbling, no complaints and no jealousy. He will find nothing but a great harmonious world around him. His mind will always be tranquil and he will be able to forgive all sinners. Therefore, the more he strives to find the way, the wider the "love that for-gives" will increase in his mind.

Fourth, Right Will and Right Concentration of mind, are relevant to the stage of "love as existence." Right Will means to plan one's future in the right way and pray for the right self-actualization. What does the right self-actualization mean for one who is seeking God's Truth? It means the completed state of a human being as a child of God. It is the state of oneness with Divinity, which we call the Nyorai state. To have Right Will is to strive for the highest state as a human being, or to become a person whose existence itself is a light for people or the object to be respected by others. That is the ultimate goal of one's life.

Right Concentration of mind, or to enter the right state of meditation, is also the highest stage for the man of religion or for one who is seeking God's Truth. Since ancient times, religious men have tried to communicate with High Divine Spirits through such forms of mental concentration as Yoga, Zen and Shikan (or introspective meditation). The first stage of the Right Concentration of mind is where one communicates with his Guardian Spirit through daily reflection. The next stage is where one communicates with his Guiding Spirit in order to fulfill his vocation. The last stage is where one communicates with the Guiding Spirits of Light in the upper realms or the Nyorai Realm.

The mind of the living human being leads to three-thousand worlds. If he can attain the state of mind as Nyorai, it will be possible for him to communicate with the Great Guiding Spirits of the Nyorai Realm through the Right Concentration of mind. There are no incarnated eight-dimensional Nyorai who are not guided directly or indirectly by the Angels of Light in the upper realms. And at the very least, they are fulfilling their heavenly mission with the help of inspiration.

In conclusion, in order to reach the stage of "love as existence," it is a prerequisite to perform Right Concentration of mind in which you meditate in a right way.

What I have stated here can be summarized as follows : Eightfold Path can be pursued in four different stages, to make the progress in your spiritual training ; Right View and Right Speech ; Right Work and Right Living ; Right Thought and Right Efforts in searching for the way ; Right Will and Right Concentration of mind.

This is similar to advancing through the stages of love that begin with the "love that loves," progress to the "love that nurtures," through the "love that forgives" and finally reach "love as existence."

Without fulfilling Right View and Right Speech, Right Work and Right Living cannot be accomplished, nor can Right Thought and Right Effort, or Right Will and Right Concentration of mind. Similarly, without the "love that loves" there cannot be the "love that nurtures," "love that forgives" or "love as existence." In short, the first stage is absolutely essential.

9. Love of Angels

So as not to limit my discussion only to the love which is received and practiced by human beings, I would like to talk about love on the supply side, which is the love of Angels in the high spiritual Realms.

Generally speaking, individuals referred to as Angels are inhabitants of the upper six-dimensional Godly Realm or higher. These consist of the various Shoten-Zenjins (Special Mission High Spirits) in the sixth dimension, Bosatsus in the seventh dimension, Nyorais in the eighth dimension, and Grand Nyorais in the ninth dimension or so-called gurus or Great Guiding Spirits of Light.

In the Real World, the ways of supplying and realizing love are all different among these Angels. The love of the six-dimensional Angels of Light consists of three different forms. The first form is love as a Guardian Tutelary for earthly people. The second is love as a Savior of Hell dwellers ; and, the third form is love as an educator of five-dimensional spiritual beings.

There are four different forms of love among the seven-dimensional Angels of Light. The first is love to guide people by incarnating on earth as a religious leader or a leader in other fields. The second is love to serve as an assistant to the Great Guiding Spirits of the Nyorai Realm. The third is love to take responsibility as a leader to save hell dwellers, and the fourth form is love as a supplier of Light from the Real World. God's Light is provided to realms of and below the sixth dimension through these Bosatsus.

There are five different forms of love among the eight-dimensional Archangels of Light. The first form is love to found a new religion on earth or to carry out a great religious reformation, to preach a new teaching by incarnating on earth every several hundred years. The second form is love as a leader of various Bosatsus. One Nyorai leads dozens of Bosatsus; accordingly, every Bosatsu has a Nyorai for a leader. The third form is love of the commander of the task force in charge of the salvation of Satan of Hell. The fourth form is love by which Archangels specialize in spreading particular rays (for example, a ray of love) that are split by the prism of God. The fifth form is creative love as a working officer in the design of new civilizations.

The love of the nine-dimensional Grand Archangels or Grand Guiding Spirits of Light includes everything, but can be roughly classified into the following six forms:

The first is love as a Messiah who incarnates on earth every several thousand years, founds a global religion and purifies the earthly world. The second is love to guide from the Real World, one who reincarnated on earth as a Messiah. The third is love to promote human evolution. The fourth is love to be the source of the seven colors of God's Light, or the love to provide a characterized Light to the eighth dimension and below. The fifth is love as the controller of order in the Real World, or love to serve as a scale by which to measure the stage of the development of people's minds. And the sixth is love as the highest commander who is ultimately responsible for the master plan for earth within the master plans of the cosmos.

10. The Great River of Love

We have so far discussed various aspects of love as human beings, as well as love as angels. Now, what is the love that flows all the way through not only the third dimension, but also the multi-dimensional worlds beyond the third dimension ? It is a rushing stream of life, an inexhaustible water of life that flows very swiftly. Actually, when I observe from the ninth-dimension all the way through to the third dimension with spiritual sight, I am awed by the magnificent panorama of the great river of love which originates at the far end of the high-dimensional world, and flows through the ninth to the third dimension as a gigantic river of energy.

Love is a great river with an irresistible force of life which flows downstream without stopping. Love has no enemies. Actually, when I behold the panoramic view of this great spiritual river of love, I clearly understand that nothing can be the enemy of love. Do you think that Hell is a force which can counter Heaven or God's World ? Or, do you think Hell is a world which is the equal counterpart of Heaven ? No is the answer. The great river named love, that sprang from God, originates at the farthest upstream and washes away everything with tremendous force. The fourth-dimensional world where the Hell Realm exists is situated all the way down at the mouth of the river. No matter how strongly the sea water salted with materialism, lust, delusions and evil tries to flow into the river, it cannot overcome the force of the unlimited current of the great river of love.

Love is light. Just as there is no darkness which can conquer light, there is no evil which can conquer love and no Hell which can defend itself forever from the great river of love. Hell is not at all a force which can counter Heaven. It is only cancerous cells which invade only a small part of the world created by God ; it is like the sea water that tries to flow into the fresh water river.

Since ancient times, Hell has been considered to be the same size as Paradise. It was also thought that Angels and Devils competed with each other. This, however, is not true. Paradise, or the Heavenly Realm, expands from the fourth- dimensional Astral Realm to the furthermost high dimensions. On the contrary, Hell is only stagnation or a dark spot, within the fourth dimension.

It is true that this stagnation is of a considerable size which accommodates several billions of Hell spirits.

However, just as ice is melted by rays of sunlight, the Hell Realm is destined to disappear eventually. The reason why the Hell Realm's influence is overestimated is that the principal region of the Hell Realm is very close to the earthly world. Consequently, these two worlds easily affect each other through vibration.

Then, what are the elements that make up the Hell Realm ? They are as follows :

Jealousy, envy, anger, grievance, an insatiable heart, complaint, pessimism, negative attitudes, indecisiveness, cowardice, laziness of mind, self-hatred, resentment, hatred for others, curse, lust, vanity, selfishness, a malicious tongue, double-dealing, manic-depression, drunken frenzies, violence, exclusiveness, lying, falsehood, materialism, atheism, solitude, dictatorship, desire for monetary gain, desire for position, desire for fame and disharmony.

All of these are negative energies. However, these negative energies are not real. Hatred, jealousy, anger and complaints are, after all, the absence of love. The problem is simply the lack of love.

After all, Hell Spirits are not powerful beings that can compete with the Light of Heaven, but are merely entities that long to be loved. In fact, Hell Spirits crave the love and kindness of people. Deep down inside them, they long for love. Therefore, Hell Spirits are actually unhappy and miserable beings whom we must save. They are afflicted with an illness called the "love deficiency" disease.

I mentioned earlier that love begins with giving.

However, souls living in the Hell Realm always want to receive, or want others to do things for them. After all, those who lived a life of the "love that deprives," without knowing the essence of love, are currently suffering in the Hell Realm. It is not too late to eliminate the Hell Realm. But how can we do this ? By having every human being understand that **THE ESSENCE OF LOVE IS IN GIVING.** What then should we begin to give ? Gratitude ! The "love that gives" begins with "thanks."

Chapter IV
The Ultimate Enlightenment
•

The Ultimate Enlightenment

•

1. What is Enlightenment?

Humankind has tirelessly sought "enlightenment" for a long time. And even though one cannot understand what enlightenment is, the desire to obtain it must include, in itself, the intention to make great strides toward self-improvement. This cannot be denied.

Enlightenment fits together well with religions and philosophies which embrace a strong fundamental desire for enlightenment. This desire, in a philosophical sense, is the attainment of Truth. It is the desire to intellectually comprehend the mysteries and structure of the world.

There is room to argue whether or not to assess "Confucianism," taught by Confucius, as a religion. However, there is no question that Confucius' teachings are one way to lead humans to the ultimate moral perfection. In short, Confucius worked to lead humans to enlightenment through the "Tao," from an educational stand point.

What I would like to stress in this chapter is mainly enlightenment in a religious sense. Of course, it encases the desire to reach a philosophical truth, and the way to perfection as a moral person. However, the most essential in religious enlightenment is that "enlightenment" is discussed in relation to Divinity.

Enlightenment is the approach to Divinity, while studying the principles of this world created by God. In this sense, there is no limit to enlightenment and there is no point at which you can say that you have "obtained enlightenment." No matter how much effort you make, it is almost impossible to conceptualize the Real World entirely. Also, it is impossible to be rewarded for one's efforts to approach Divinity before the elapse of an infinite amount of time.

However, it is also true that there are various stages in enlightenment. Therefore, it is possible for you to reach a particular level of enlightenment, as there exists the highest level of enlightenment for a human in flesh on the ground. I would like to explain the steps toward this highest possible enlightenment.

Among the greatest religious leaders or Gurus, who are still remembered by our contemporaries and who sought "enlightenment" most rigorously, was Gautama Siddhartha, or Shakyamuni, who taught the Truth in India two thousand five hundred and several tens of years ago. Various books have been written about the refinement of Shakyamuni's enlightenment since he was first enlightened under a pipal tree, until he passed away at age eighty under a sala tree outside the town of Kushinagara in contemporary Northeast India. However, most of those books describe the facts only as thoughts ; the books don't describe the actual state of enlightenment.

The world of the mind is full of wonder. Since I opened the door of my mind and became able to communicate with my subconscious, already nine years have elapsed. During this period, I became able to comprehend the things that saints of the past have thought, done, deliberated and conceptualized as if they were my own experiences. The world of the mind is truly mysterious.

I can perceive the enlightenment that Shakyamuni attained under a pipal tree as if it were right before my eyes. Although it happened to him two thousand and several hundreds of years ago, I can realize it as if it were happening now.

In this chapter, I would like to review what enlightenment means in the context of the modern world, focusing mainly on Shakyamuni's enlightenment. I wish to impart my knowledge of enlightenment for future people because methodologies for enlightenment are legacies from the human past and hope for humans of the future.

2. Enlightenment as Grace

For what are we humans trying to attain enlighten-ment ? If one managed to achieve it, what on earth could one get from it ? Before thinking about this, we first need to consider the original purpose and mission of human beings.

The fundamental questions are, "Why were we human beings born into this world ?" and, "Why are we humans born into flesh ?"

In heaven, before we were born as humans, we used to enjoy absolutely unrestrained lives as spirits. In Heaven, we would never starve to death ; we would never live on the street because we had no money ; we need not suffer in our mother's wombs for nine months, nor constantly cry and be ignorant as chil-dren. There is no difficulty related to sex in adoles-cence, nor conflicts between parents and children. No economic difficulties ; no pain over serving other peo-ple in the office ; no stress over having to meet nasty people, nor the grief of being parted from beloved ones. There is no sorrow in becoming old, nor the misery of illness. Moreover, there is no fear of becoming ugly ; no misery over being abandoned by children or grand-children ; no grief from being parted from a spouse by death, nor the fret that we will eventually die. Heaven is where no such afflictions exist.

Chapter IV : The Ultimate Enlightenment

In Heaven, everyone's mind is transparent. And those with disharmonious minds cannot exist with the others in the same world. Therefore, the people whom you meet everyday are wonderful and absolutely compatible with you. It is the world where everybody loves and nurtures each other.

Spiritual beings there can decide their own age, and can make appear anything they desire. Those people strive to train their souls at their own individual stages in order to become more awakened to God's Truth.

Disharmonious spirits down in the Hell Realm can never be born on the earth as humans. Their minds are so full of fight and destruction that they are never permitted to incarnate into a human body.

Then, what should they do in order to transmigrate to this world on the earth. At least, they are required to qualify for the four-dimensional Posthumous Realm (Astral Realm). Unless they understand that they are spiritual existences and the children of God well enough to be inhabitants of Heaven, they are not permitted to be reborn on earth. Therefore, unless they complete a minimum amount of required reflections, they cannot transmigrate.

Thus, transmigration to the earth, itself, is a trial from the very beginning for those who dwelled in Heaven. For a spirit who has finally completed necessary reflections after a long period spent in the Hell Realm, it is a chance to restart as a human being and relive a life on the ground.

In short, the earthly world is a sort of training

ground. For spirits who lived in perfect freedom in the Heavenly world, incarnating into flesh is a trial for them to test their spirituality and divine nature. Earth is the place where one can thoroughly test the genuineness of his own spiritual awakening. It is easy to believe in God when one enjoys perfect spiritual freedom. To what extent can one understand the rules of the Real World while he lives under the rules of the material world? Can one realize the power of God? Can one understand that the power of God is always working in this world? These points are tested on earth, and only after a human being has thoroughly passed the tests can he return to the Real World, and advance to a higher realm than the one he originated from before his incarnation.

There is the type of spirit who, after experiencing a long period of suffering in Hell, reaches the introspective state of mind where he can obtain the minimum level of enlightenment necessary for a human being to realize that he is a child of God. Then, this spirit is incarnated on this earth, this time with the determination to be an excellent person. However, seriously influenced by the negative vibrations of the three-dimensional world, some spirits can never return to the Heavenly world, but fall into an even deeper Hell. Such spirits indulge in the world of lust without realizing that they are actually children of God.

This three-dimensional material world (or the phenomenal world) can be regarded as a place of severe training. On the other hand, it also offers one a chance for salvation. People who never have the opportunity to meet each other in the Real World, can do so in this three-dimensional world. Therefore, living in this world offers people a great chance to meet the Great Guiding Spirits of Light in flesh as well as people whose minds are attuned to Satan of Hell. These people start from the same line, are born with a mewl and are given an equal chance to live their lives over again. In other words, the grace of enlightenment is in the chance to live one's life over again.

3. Methods for Enlightenment

Now, the next problem is how a human being can attain enlightenment. Enlightenment means further refinement of one's spiritual or divine nature in a fresh course of one's life. When you think about the methods to refine the nature, you may notice that there are various possibilities and an unlimited number of ways.

Various possibilities means various training methods. Not only Buddhism but also Christianity, Shintoism, Confucianism, Taoism and Islam offer their own methodologies of training. However, these methods often lead living people to get lost in a forest instead of approaching Divinity. And people would consequently wonder which religion is genuine instead of which method of training is best.

Every global religion represents God's Light in some way or another. In the religions which have impressed people's minds for hundreds or thousands of years, the lives of leaders' have the brilliance of God's Light which never ceases to warrant people's respect. I must point out though, that each Light has a different color in accordance with the period, ethnic and climatic origin of each religion.

However, let's leave past teachings in the past. New teachings are needed now for the coming ages. It is an urgent requirement that new teachings emerge and new methods of training be sought.

The methods for enlightenment are the "guidelines" by which to merge one's state of mind with Divinity. They show us how to live life in line with the mind of God. Those are the ways to seek a life in line with God's Truth.

One way is the Genuine Eightfold Path and another is the Theory of Staged Development of Love. For those who seek the way through Buddhism, the Genuine Eightfold Path can guide an everyday life since it includes the universal God's Truth. And the way to become a complete human, which is an endless process.

How many people on earth can see and speak in a right way ? How many people can work and live in a right manner ? And, how many have thoroughly mastered the deepest truth of Buddhism; to concentrate one's mind, with good intention, in a right manner ? Thus, the Genuine Eightfold Path is a practical method for enlightenment, which cannot be mastered thoroughly in one's lifetime.

It must at least take five to ten years to master how to see and speak rightly. If you think you have achieved this, try to spend everyday of your life concentrating on working and living rightly. If you can achieve that, perhaps you have obtained the enlightenment of the six-dimensional Godly Realm.

When you manage to think rightly and make efforts to approach the truth in a right way and establish a state of mind in which you can survive through any difficulties in your life with an unshakable mind, you have reached the state of Arahan (Arahat in Sanskrit). The state of Arahan is the gateway to advancement from the six-dimensional Godly Realm to the seven-dimensional Bosatsu Realm ; the state where a relevant level of self-establishment is accomplished. If you are disturbed by the petty comments of others, become furious over trivial problems, or seduced by the desire for important positions or honor, you cannot claim to have reached the state of Arahan.

Nowadays, there are innumerable religious leaders everywhere in the world, including Japan - take a good look at their minds and hearts as well as their deeds. The ones who become angry when their words are criticized, or others who threaten their disciples with life in Hell or punishment unless they give money, have never achieved the Arahan state. The state of Arahan is the initial step to becoming an Angel of Light. If one's mind is tempted by the desire for important positions or honor, money, sensuality, anger, resentment or regrets, he can never qualify as a natural religious leader.

The basic method to obtain enlightenment is to set your target at the Arahan state, in which you are not disturbed by worldly matters, your mind and heart are always clear and calm, and you can communicate with your Guardian Spirit and can understand other people's minds as clearly as your own. Without achieving this stage, you cannot advance toward higher levels of training or enlightenment. So, you should first aim at the Arahan state. And the state of genuine awakening through God's Truth will unfold itself thereafter.

4. Nyoshin

What is profound enlightenment ? What is the state beyond that of Arahan ?

At one's Arahan state, a firm faith in Divinity is established, his mind cannot be shaken by worldly troubles. He lives every day under the guidance of his Guardian Spirit and he can see other people's minds as clearly as his own. This is a stage close to completion as a human being ; he is ready to guide ordinary people as a man of religion.

However, there still remains the danger of degradation at the Arahan state as one can only communicate with his own Guardian Spirit in his subconscious, but cannot sufficiently understand the mind of high spirits. He hasn't come to the stage where he can see the altitude, the variety or the depth of different teachings about the Truth. Therefore, he is at risk of being misled by extraordinary or vicious teachings.

For example, after a genuine religious leader dies, often each of his disciples begins to speak individually, eventually causing the group to split up. This may well take place when the disciples who once achieved the Arahan state so easily follow the way to degradation, having lost a proper balance of mind. The reason why those who achieved a respectable level of enlightenment through a particular method of training may become deluded is that they are not prepared to cope with other sorts of teachings or methods of training.

In another case, people who learned the teachings of mind from a respectable teacher may be attracted to spiritual phenomena such as spiritual healing or the worship of supernatural powers after the leader's death. This occurs because a proper "scale of mind," which can measure different sorts of teachings, is not yet established.

There is yet another reason one can degrade from the Arahan state. The Arahan state can be compared to the metal which shines radiantly after the rust on its surface is removed. However, because anticorrosive is not applied to the surface, it is easy for rust to develop again, unless the soul is constantly polished. Therefore, if one is satisfied with being called "great master," without noticing that his soul is again starting to rust, he will have many problems.

When one's soul shines radiantly, the surface is so smooth that it can repel any attack of evil notions; once the soul gets rusty, the surface gets rough enough for such thoughts to stick.

There exist entities who hammer pitons into this surface and, on these, hang climbing ropes. These entities are the Devils of Hell. On these ropes which extend all the way to Hell, creatures of the dark world can climb upwards. They are ghosts, animal spirits and devils.

Thus, some religious teachers who once achieved the Arahan state may overlook the demons who intrude their minds. He then deludes the general public and leads them to madness. This is the most dangerous trap.

Therefore, it is essential to remove the rust from the soul—to polish it thoroughly to prevent the rust from developing. If your soul has rough spots like rust, it is under constant threat of being attacked by demons with their hooks and climbing rope.

No matter how you try to stop these demons, another batch will attack from behind. There is no countermeasure against this situation. Mere spiritual purification or exorcism can never save you, in the true sense.

Make your soul shine. It is essential to polish your soul. And if possible, you should apply anticorrosive to your soul. This will lead it to a higher stage of enlightenment.

Chapter IV : The Ultimate Enlightenment

The state of enlightenment higher than Arahan is called "Nyoshin." Nyoshin is the stage where you can receive guidance from a more highly graded spiritual realm than that of your own Guardian Spirit, or the stage where you can communicate with your Guiding Spirit. The Guiding Spirits belong to higher realms, from the seven-dimensional Bosatsu Realm onward. The state of Nyoshin is almost irreversible, so it is almost impossible for demonic creatures to intrude into one's mind because, with the guidance of Nyorais and Bosatsus, it radiates too strong a light for demons to approach.

At the Nyoshin stage, one's mind and heart are always modest and unassuming ; it is preoccupied with how it can serve the world or save deluded people. The major cause of degradation from the Arahan state is conceit. But at this Nyoshin state, any selfishness or self-indulgence disappears and the mind remains calm. Beginning at the Nyoshin state one becomes able to practice "Right Will" and "Right Concentration" of mind, in a true sense.

Nyoshin has yet another aspect. As the state of mind approaches the Kan-Jizai state (literally, unrestricted vision), you can see anything about a person who is even hundreds of kilometers away from you. For example, just seeing a certain person's name, you can tell the person's current condition of mind, concerns, haunting spirit, previous life, two lives before, three lives before or future life, in an instant. This state is near the completion of a seeker's enlightenment.

5. Kan-Jizai

Nyoshin is comparable to the state of Bosatsu in which one has opened his Spiritual Path (see chapter VI for details). Nyoshin can also be the enlightenment of Nyorais. Nyoshin has different levels, but usually the Nyoshin, one step above Arahan, means the state of Bosatsu. It is not only the case for the ones who attained enlightenment in the Earthly Realm, but also applicable to the spirits in the other world, or the Real World.

It is not correct to assume that spirits in the next world understand everything. The range of a spirit's ability to understand and grasp things depends on the level of cognition and enlightenment which that spirit has attained. A typical example is "precognition." Every spirit in the Real World beyond the third dimension can foresee, to some extent, what will happen in the future. However, problems arise when some precognitive information is conveyed to people in the three-dimensional world. There often occurs some discrepancy in time and place.

To expand on this point, there are two reasons for the discrepancy. The first point is that future events are partly definite and partly fluid. The definite events are already decided in the high spiritual world and can not be reversed. On the other hand, the fluid events are at an indefinite stage, or are the belief that a natural course will lead to such and such events. Therefore, these events can be changed through the efforts of people on earth or their Guardian and Guiding Spirits. Thus, the foresight of the spirits of Heaven is not always accurate or realized.

The second reason is that the accuracy of the foresight varies depending upon the grades of the spirits' consciousness and the areas of their speciality. Generally speaking, the higher the spiritual grade, the more accurate foresight becomes. Also, specialists can achieve a higher level of accuracy as they are spirits who are specifically specialized in foreseeing as a vocation.

Now, I would like to explain the state of Kan-Jizai which is above Nyoshin.

At the beginning of a Buddhist scripture named *Han-nya Shin-gyo*, a sentence reads *"Kan-Jizai Bosatsu Gyojin Hannya Haramitaji."* A direct translation is, "When Kan-Jizai Bosatsu progressed remarkably in his spiritual trainings and opened the treasury of his subconscious...." Kan-Jizai Bosatsu is not a person's name. It signifies the state of Bosatsu where one reaches a stage of Kan-Jizai as a result of progress in his trainings.

Bosatsu is a phase of mind where one has completed the stage of "Lesser Vehicle," or establishment of oneself, and prepares for the stage of "Great Vehicle," or standing up for the salvation of the general public. However, even in a Bosatsu state, one may have

125

humanistic afflictions and pains which prevent him from performing divine power at any time. As he progresses enough as a Bosatsu to reach the state of enlightenment of the upper part of the Bosatsu Realm, or Bonten's state, he becomes capable of performing supernatural powers on a stable basis regardless of illness, unexpected occurrences or conflicts in human relationships. Thus, Kan-Jizai Bosatsu is the state of Bonten, or the spirit which advances to the spiritual demand on the boundary between the Bosatsu and Nyorai Realms, described as the seventh and at the same time the eighth dimensions.

A Kan-Jizai Bosatsu was called Apporokishti Shbar-ah at the time of Shakyamuni in India. It is a stage to be endowed with all the six great supernatural powers, if not sufficient. The six great supernatural powers are, "Tengen" (literally, heaven eyes), "Tenji" (heaven ears), "Tashin" (others' minds), "Sukumei" (fate), "Shinsoku" (god's foot) and "Rojin" (concealed potency). Next, I would like to explain each of these powers.

"Tengen" (clairvoyance) is the ability of spiritual sight. It enables one to see the aura or haunting evil spirits of living humans. A man with this ability can also view the other world, or the Real World.

"Tenji" (clairaudience) is the ability to hear the voices of the spirits in the next world. Trance speech, or the ability to speak spirits' words, is also included in this power.

"Tashin" (telepathy) is the ability to read minds.

Mind reading ; the ability to understand other people's minds as clearly as your own.

"Sukumei" is the ability to know not only one's own "future, but also the fate of others, by reading the thought belt" of others. (One's past thoughts and deeds are recorded in the thought belt of one's mind). By means of this power, one can, of course, know about one's former lives.

"Shinsoku" is what is called astral travel. It is an out-of-body experience in which one explores the spiritual world or teleports himself to different places.

"Rojin" is the state of mind of Confucius, who declared, "I follow my own aspiration and yet do not surpass the rules"; the ability to live an ordinary person's life while possessing a high level of supernatural powers. It is the state of a great saint in a town, not that of a small saint hidden in the mountains.

Kan-Jizai Bosatsu is a person in a state in which the above mentioned six great supernatural powers are, to some extent, mastered. It is one step higher than "Nyoshin" where one can read many people's minds simultaneously or the mind of a person who is far away.

6. One Is Many ; Many Are One

I would like to talk about enlightenment at the stage where Right Thought, Right Efforts, Right Will and

Right Concentration of Mind are deepened to the maximum in the course of a human's spiritual training, and where one reaches the phase of "love as existence," according to the Theory of the Staged Development of Love. In short, I would like to explain the enlightenment of the Nyorai Realm itself.

Until the stage of Bosatsu, the recognition of a soul is affected to some extent by the physical appearance of the human being. A spirit is originally formless energy, or a shapeless intellect. However, because they have experienced innumerable lives as humans, many spirits are restricted by the idea of a soul in the shape of a human and have almost lost intrinsic freedom in terms of their function.

Still in the seven-dimensional Bosatsu Realm, spirits undertake training in the shape of humans. A human being has two arms, two legs, clothes to wear, a certain hairdo or facial features; the majority of Bosatsus can only recognize themselves by these features. They do not feel at ease unless in the shape of a human being, even in the other world. So, although they are highly virtuous and endowed with a high level of leadership, they are still restricted by the spiritual ability of humans.

However, up in the eight-dimensional Nyorai Realm, the situation becomes different. Habitants of the Nyorai Realm know that they are not souls in the shape of human beings. The shape is, for them, only a memory of once being lodged in human flesh during a long process of transmigration. Also, Nyorais know and recognize not only intrinsically, but also through actual, everyday situations, that a spirit is an energy body with an intellect, or a shapeless bundle of light.

For instance, what would a psychic living on the ground see if he were to separate from his body to travel to the eight-dimensional Nyorai Realm as a spirit ? To the person belonging to the Earthly Realm, Nyorais in the eighth dimension would present themselves in the figure they used on the ground, to be easily recognized by the person from the ground. Then they would take him to their houses and serve coffee or wine that tastes more delicious and flavorful than anyone on the ground could ever imagine. Then the psychic visitor from the earthly world would report as follows :

"The eight-dimensional Nyorai Realm is really wonderful. The habitants there all look divine. The roads are covered with rubies and the buildings are decorated with diamonds. The drinks there have a dreamy flavor which could never be found on the ground. Tables are made of glorious marble and the pillars in the four corners of the room are of crystals which can only be described as marvelous."

Emmanuel Swedenborg, a famous modern-age European psychic, must have reported in this manner. However, it shows how insufficient his abilities of spiritual recognition are. If he had watched the scene more carefully, the roads or buildings decorated with gem stones would have disappeared and there would have been only a Nyorai standing there with a wide smile on his face. If he had concentrated further with his spiritual sight, even the Nyorai would have disappeared and only a great globe of light would have remained. Such rubies or diamonds are transformed into three-dimensions to please the visitor from the Earthly Realm.

Thus, the enlightenment of the Nyorai Realm reaches the stage where one can recognize himself as a shapeless entity. Therefore, if there are people who attained enlightenment as Nyorai while living on the earth, they must be aware of the rule of the Nyorai Realm.

The rule of the Nyorai Realm is "One is many, many are one." This means that in the Nyorai Realm, the number "one" cannot exist by objective recognition. The "one" can be "ten" or "ten thousand"; the "one thousand" can be "one." There exists not an objective fact, but the absolute existence, or as many beings as the number of the functions of consciousness ; only the consciousness which takes full control of all of these knows the reality.

Let's put it simply. If there are ten jobs that a Nyorai must do, he appears as ten, if there are ten thousand such jobs, he can appear as ten thousand. At the same time, even though he appears to be divided into ten thousand, there is still only one unifying consciousness which recognizes these ten thousand as one.

A Kyoto school philosopher who lived in Japan in recent years, Kitaro Nishida, appears to have understood this Nyorai Realm rule as a result of his philosophical studies. Of course, it is also true that his subconsciousness taught him the existence of such a world, as he himself was originally from the Nyorai Realm.

The eighth dimension is the world where absolute contradictions can be resolved. The world where visually separate and contradictory beings can converge through intuitive unification. The philosopher Kitaro Nishida had apparently attained the enlightenment of this Nyorai Realm while he was still alive.

7. The Enlightenment of the Sun Realm

The enlightenment of the Nyorai Realm is that of "one is many, many are one," which is beyond the senses of human flesh. It is to be awakened to the fact that a spirit is a portion of God's Light, a shapeless energy body, or intelligence without form. This stage of enlightenment is about as much as a living human can attain. The population of the terrestrial spirit group is several tens of billions ; of these, less than five hundred live in the eight-dimensional Nyorai Realm. This fact indicates how difficult the enlightenment of the Nyorai Realm is to obtain.

The enlightenment of Nyorai is at the stage of unification, or sublimation beyond the dualism of virtue and vice. It is not enough to polish oneself in simple training in life to obtain this enlightenment. It also requires clear reason and an understanding deep enough to comprehend and master the grand drama and Laws of the Cosmos.

What sort of people from the eighth-dimensional Nyorai Realm were born in Japan? Aside from the mythical ages, one was Shotoku Taishi, around the age of the Taika Revolution. Also, a Heian Period priest, Kukai, and Kamakura Period priest, Nichiren. In the Showa Period (1926 AD—1989 AD), the previously mentioned Kitaro Nishida, and Masaharu Taniguchi, the founder of Seicho-no-Ie, are also examples. There were a few more in addition to these five.

The eight-dimensional Nyorai Realm, populated by just below five hundred Nyorais, can be divided into four levels. The lowest is the upper part of a state called the Bonten Realm, in which there are about forty Nyorais. Above this is the level called Semi Divine Realm which is populated by one hundred and twenty. Above this is called Light Divine Realm which is populated by about two hundred eighty. The highest of the eight-dimensional Nyorai Realm is called the Sun Realm in a narrow sense ; in a broader sense, the Sun Realm includes the nine-dimensional Cosmic Realm. The Sun Realm in a narrow sense is populated by about twenty Grand Nyorais, who are positioned between the eighth and ninth dimensions.

Who are those Grand Nyorais in this Sun Realm? From Japanese Shintoism, three gods, namely, Ame-no-Minakanushi-no-Kami (the Lord God of the Heav-

Chapter IV : The Ultimate Enlightenment

enly Center), Ame-no-Tokotachi-no-Kami and
Kanmi-Musubi-no-Kami, are there. Seven Archangels
from Christianity including the Chief Archangel,
Michael, live there. Lao-tzu of Taoism and Mo-tzu of
Moism are there. Apollo from Greek mythology and
the Greek philosophers, Socrates and Plato are also
there. From Buddhism, Dainichi Nyorai (Mahavairocana in Sanskrit), Amida Nyorai and other Nyorai,
live there. Mohammed of Islam seems to dwell in the
Light Divine Realm, one level below the Sun Realm.

Now, what are the common features of the
"enlightenment of the Sun Realm" which were attained
by the habitants of that realm?

In short, it is not an enlightenment of a human being
any more. It is beyond the state that a human being
can reach through personal efforts. These people are
endowed with Divinity.

The Sun Realm is already beyond the reach of
human training. The habitants there are already
Grand Divine Spirits. They can establish their own
individual religion and become fundamental gods of
that religion.

What is the basis that supports the idea that their
enlightenment is beyond the reach of human beings?
In short, they are directly involved in the master plan
for the evolution of the terrestrial human race. Those
spirits from the Sun Realm assist the spirits of the nine-
dimensional Cosmic Realm in making projects, drawing plans, and carry them out to develop particular
civilizations, to restore religions, or to bring the wave of

a new age on earth. Sometimes they are born directly on the ground to work, like Leonardo da Vinci (Archangel Gabriel) or Martin Luther (Archangel Michael), but usually they stay and work in Heaven.

8. The Enlightenment of Shakyamuni (1) Grand Enlightenment

Before discussing the enlightenment of the nine-dimensional Cosmic Realm, let me tell you about the enlightenment which Gautama Siddhartha or Shakyamuni attained in India two thousand and several hundreds of years ago.

Shakyamuni embraced a religious life when he was twenty-nine years old. It was at the age of thirty-five that he attained enlightenment under a pipal tree, renouncing the asceticism he had pursued for six years. Early one morning around one o'clock, he went into a deep trance after completing about a week's reflective meditation. He obtained the following enlightenment :

"I have pursued asceticism for many years believing that I could obtain a great spiritual leap or enlightenment after tormenting my body to the maximum by not eating or drinking properly."

"Since six years ago when I abandoned my wife, Yashodhara, and my son, Rahula, declined my father Shuddhodana's wish to succeed him and fled the Castle at Kapilavastu, I experienced six rounds of four seasons. I had a strong muscular body and was equally distinguished as a soldier and a scholar when I was at Kapilavastu. Look at me now ! My ribs stand out, my eyes are deeply sunken and my body looks like a mere skeleton."

"If tormenting the flesh is what training in life is all about, isn't it a mistake for a human being to be born lodged in flesh in the first place ? If Divinity wishes for us to deny our flesh, suicide must be the best enlightenment."

"However, what will we gain by committing suicide ? The Law of the Macrocosm lies in the unlimited chain of cause and effect, and it is certain that we will harvest evil crops if we plant evil seeds. If we create a new cause of affliction through suicide, an absolutely intolerable affliction will be waiting for us in Hell. Isn't asceticism and the torment of one's body nothing more than a slow suicide ?"

"If the state of Divinity is tranquillity, it doesn't exist in asceticism. No seed of enlightenment can be found within asceticism. What I have obtained after six years' severe training is frightening, ugly looks and piercing eyes that threaten people. The only thing one can obtain through asceticism is severity. Severe eyes which shoot other people like an arrow do not bear any love or mercy."

"Unless my mind itself is in peace and filled with happiness, how can I be genuinely gentle and considerate to others ?"

"But, what is a sense of happiness within myself ?

When I was in the castle of Kapilavastu as a prince, satiated by everybody and everything including money, women and material goods, was I filled with happiness ?"

"No, what I found there was only boredom ; my soul was always afflicted with hunger and thirst. Amid the entanglements of various people's thoughts, my mind was constantly restless with discord. My future was to succeed the throne. I would have had to lead the people of Kapilavastu to fight neighboring countries. There was to be much bloodshed."

"Seeking worldly position or honor gave me only emptiness. My days at Kapilavastu were never happy for me. I was frustrated spiritually and my uneasiness mounted day by day. The happiness of human beings is not found in stagnation and inertia. It lies in the daily progress of the spirit. Worldly success doesn't offer it. The genuine happiness of human beings born as children of God is found only in the progress of one's own spiritual and divine nature, in accordance with the mind of God."

"The genuine enlightenment and happiness of a human being as a child of God is not found in an extravagant life at a palace nor in extreme asceticism. No true enlightenment, happiness, or peace of mind can be found either in a life which indulges the flesh to an extreme, or a life which torments the flesh to an extreme."

"The genuine life of a human being is the one that seeks the Truth in the Middle Way, abandoning the extremes of the right and left. The Middle Way is only found in a balanced life as a human being ; there emerges a grand harmony, absolutely free of affliction and indulgence."

"What a human being seeks for from the bottom of his heart, is the world of grand harmony. The true kingdom of mind or the true land of Buddha will emerge only if everybody follows the Middle Way, abandons extreme affliction and indulgence, and practices the Eightfold Path. This consists of Right View, Right Thought, Right Speech, Right Work, Right Living, Right Effort, Right Will and Right Concentration of Mind."

"True human happiness lies in daily spiritual joy and spiritual improvement. Only in the pursuit and realization of the profundity of the Eightfold Path can one enhance his sense of happiness."

9. The Enlightenment of Shakyamuni (2)
Passing Away

In the previous section I portrayed Shakyamuni's state of mind when he attained great enlightenment at the age of thirty-five. The description of Shakyamuni's enlightenment, two thousand five hundred years ago, unrolled itself in front of me in letters written by my automatically moving pen. However, the details of his enlightenment would fill an entire volume.

So, I've decided to omit what he taught for forty-five years, but instead, in the form of his very words, show you the enlightenment or state of mind that Shakyamuni obtained as he was passing away at the age of eighty. Under a sala tree in Kusinagara, laying on his right side, his right arm folded under his head, and his left hand on his aching stomach, Shakyamuni was entering nirvana, as he thought the following :

"Since I obtained an initial enlightenment at the age of thirty-five, I have been teaching the true ways of Divinity for forty-five years. However, I seem to be approaching the moment when I have to leave my flesh. Thank you very much, my withered body, for serving me for as long as eighty years. Thanks to your perseverance, I could preach the Truth to people and show them the way to live as human beings. My organs, I really appreciate your service."

"My disciples, thank you very much for all those years. I appreciate all your efforts, from your daily care of me, to your spreading of the Laws. Thanks to you, the Shakyamuni Order has grown rather large with five thousand followers. I don't know how many hundreds of thousands of people there are throughout Yojana, throughout India, who believe in my teachings. All of those were made possible because you kept spreading God's Truth, fighting against religious persecution and outmaneuvering religious enemies. Without all of you, my teachings would not have had much strength. Thank you very much."

"Shariputra, you passed away some years ago. I look

forward to seeing you again in the other world so we may talk face to face again. I really appreciate your past efforts. As you were a good listener, it was easy for me to give speeches. Sometimes, you asked me stupid questions which made me laugh, but many people who didn't dare to ask me directly appreciated your questions !"

"Yasa, how many women wanted to become nuns just because I had a fair, good-looking man like you as a disciple ! How much I regretted having you as a disciple when I saw women shaving their hair, abandoning their homes and asking for my acceptance while I received complaints from their parents ! Now you, too, have become a good old man. As I am to be born again in an Eastern country in my next life, be sure to be born at the same time and help me work. Please, don't forget it !"

"Ananda, you are still young and you haven't obtained remarkable spiritual abilities yet. But you will soon reach the state of Arahan. As you have an extraordinary memory, remember well what I have taught, and make a big contribution when scriptures are compiled."

"Upali, you were always short-tempered and quick to fight. When someone criticized me, you used to roll up your sleeves and strike at the person. You really had a sense of righteousness. In your next life, you will seek the Lotus Sutra in an Eastern country. At that time, you shouldn't attack the other sects too much."

"Maitreya, even though you are a woman, you have

kept up with my teachings very well. When I am reborn in an Eastern country, you will also transmigrate in the same era. It seems you will be born ahead of me and will act as my herald. Be sure to include in the scriptures that I will transmigrate to an Eastern country."

"Oh, thinking about my beloved disciples, I am so concerned about them after I leave this world. My disciples, remember well. My life will soon leave the earth, but the teachings I left will remain for thousands of years and give food to people's minds."

"My soul-related disciples, remember my last words very well. My life is like the full moon. Even if the moon seems to disappear into clouds, it is still shining radiantly behind them. Likewise, a life shines eternally. It will never ever end."

"From now on, even after I pass away, be sure to live with what I have taught for forty-five years as food for your mind. With my teachings as nourishment for your mind, light up your own mind and illuminate your way—don't depend on anybody else. With the Light of Truth in your mind, live a steady life. What I have long taught you is to first establish yourself, and then save others."

"Even after my death, do not forget to lighten up yourself and live a strong, righteous, honest and cheerful life. Thank you very much indeed for such a long period of time."

Such were the thoughts that Shakyamuni had as he passed away. Even Shakyamuni could barely speak when he was dying, so the disciples with their spiritual paths open, heard spiritually the teacher's voice of mind and left it as the Nirvana Scripture.

10. The Enlightenment of the Ninth Dimension

The enlightenment of Shakyamuni, as well as those of Moses and Jesus Christ, was the highest enlightenments that humankind has ever reached. However, even his forty-five years' efforts couldn't have taught his disciples the enlightenment of the Macrocosm Shakyamuni understood. Even as disciples of Buddha, almost none of them could obtain an enlightenment of Nyorai ; it was too hard for Shakyamuni to teach them about the creation, or the dimensional structure of the Macrocosm.

Moreover, at the time, India was in a constant state of battle, Shakyamuni couldn't have saved people's souls if he were to preach teachings which surpassed the framework of that age. Therefore, he focused on elevating people's minds to the state of Arahan through the Eightfold Path.

Essentially, the enlightenment of the nine-dimensional Cosmic Realm must satisfy the following three conditions :

1) To obtain all-round laws so that one may teach anybody under any circumstances.

2) To be enlightened about genesis ; the creation of the

Cosmos and the history of the Earth.

3) To have been enlightened about the structure of multi-dimensional universes, starting from the fourth dimension.

To teach any one under any circumstances as mentioned in 1, was what Shakyamuni was very good at. The enlightenment related to genesis mentioned in 2, was what he had attained under the pipal tree when he had a mysterious "Experience of Cosmic Consciousness." He recognized that his spiritual body had expanded infinitely in the Cosmos; the Grand Enlightenment. Enlightenment about the Laws of the Cosmos and the Real World mentioned in 3, was expressed as the laws of cause and effect or the laws of karma.

Of course, nine-dimensional enlightenment is accompanied with all six divine supernatural powers at maximum strength, and the ability to see through past, present and future lives. However, Shakyamuni immediately foresaw the danger of seekers of God's Truth worshipping supernatural powers. In order to warn them against delusion, he hardly used any powers other than mind-reading.

I have already mentioned in Chapter I that there are ten supreme Grand Guiding Spirits of Light with nine-dimensional enlightenment. The description of the role of each one, at present, is as follows :

1) Shakyamuni—Creation of a new century and construction of a new civilization.

2) Jesus Christ—Determination of Heaven's guiding

strategy.

3) Confucius—Planning of the terrestrial spirit group's evolution program.

4) El Ranty—Personnel.

5) Moses—Head of activities to remove Hell.

6) Manu—Racial problems.

7) Maitrayer—Putting God's light into prisms.

8) Newton—Science and technology.

9) Zeus—Fine arts such as music, visual art and literature.

10) Zoroaster—Moral perfection.

Of these ten, the group of five from Shakyamuni to Moses are upper nine-dimensional spirits who take charge of decision making for the terrestrial spirit group. Among this group, three spirits namely Shakyamuni, Jesus Christ and El Ranty seem to have chaired the board in turn.

El Ranty recently incarnated on earth. He was then called Shinji Takahashi, who headed a Japanese religious body, GLA (God Light Association). As it has not been long since he returned to the Real World, he has not resumed leadership in the ninth dimension. However, when Shakyamuni and Jesus Christ were born on the ground, El Ranty acted as the chairman of the ninth dimension.

At present Jesus Christ is in charge of decision making as the chief executive. He is scheduled to reincarnate on earth about four hundred years from now. At that time, what are now the waters of Bermuda will upheave to form the New Atlantis Continent, including present-day Canada. And the southern half of present-day North America will sink into the ocean. At present, Jesus Christ is planned to reincarnate in the New Atlantis Continent. In that land Jesus will teach God's Truth based on the principles of love and rightness suitable for the cosmic age.

In this chapter, I have discussed enlightenment up to the nine-dimensional world. Of course on top of this exists enlightenment of the tenth dimension. However, as the ten-dimensional consciousnesses are three planetary consciousnesses, namely, Grand Sun Consciousness, Moon Consciousness and the Earth Consciousness, we can exclude the enlightenment of the tenth dimension if we define the enlightenment under study as that of spirits who may incarnate on earth. Ten-dimensional enlightenment is not of the Humanistic Realm. In short, a ten-dimensional existence is a great mass of light with a particular purpose.

Chapter V
The Golden Age

•

The Golden Age

•

1. Omens Foretelling A New Breed of Humankind

As we are now living in the latter half of the twentieth century, the twenty-first century is close at hand. What kinds of people will emerge with the coming of the new age ? And what kind of age will it be ? I suppose that many people today are filled with expectation and anxiety as they look forward to the next century.

Omens foretelling the emergence of a new age and a new breed of humankind are already visible in present-day society. The current age is actually a boundary between the time when many old things perish and many new things eventually spring forth. Accordingly, the bud of the new age exists today. It is the mission of prophets like ourselves to reveal these things to the people of the present day.

Humankind observed the destruction of the old civilization when Atlantis sank into the ocean some ten thousand years ago. And as the end of one thing means the start of another, after the destruction of Atlantis a new civilization developed, centered around Egypt. This civilization has lasted for about ten thousand years, but will cease to be at the end of the twentieth century.

Over the past ten thousand years, various civilizations have flourished in many regions and countries, starting with Egypt, then moving on to Persia, Israel, China, Europe, the Americas and Japan. The main characteristic of the current civilization is its emphasis on the concept of "intelligence." Throughout this age of intellect, numerous attempts have been made to understand the world intellectually.

The preceding civilization of Atlantis was based on the concept of "reason," and in the nine-dimensional Cosmic Realm, Maitrayer and Koot Hoomy, who was later known as Archimedes and still later as Isaac Newton, were extremely active and prominent during this time.

Before Atlantis, there existed the Mu continent in the Pacific Ocean some fifteen thousand years ago. The Mu civilization was quite peculiar as it was one of light energy. During this age, scientific and religious studies on light energy were quite advanced, and the cultivation and training of individual's centered around learning how to amplify their own individual light power.

Further back in history, we come to the continent of Lemuria, which was located in the Indian Ocean over thirty-seven thousand years ago. Humankind of the Lemurian age was mainly concerned with the concept of "sensitivity." El Ranty and El Cantare (who later incarnated as Buddha) were quite influential in the age of Mu. Manu and Zeus, who led the creation of the civilization of sensitivity, were extremely active in the age of Lemuria.

Training in life for the people of Lemuria was based on their own level of sensitivity and, indeed, the most cultivated Lemurians could distinguish between three thousand different colors and two thousand-five hundred different smells.

Before the advent of the Lemurian civilization came that of Myutram, which flourished on the continent of Myutram and disappeared a hundred and fifty-three thousand years ago. At that time the position of the earth's axis was quite different from today. Present-day Antarctica, where the continent of Myutram was located, was in the temperate zone. The shape of the Myutram continent was, however, a bit different from that of Antarctica. Myutram did not sink into the ocean, as did Mu and Atlantis. Rather, a shift in the earth's axis made Myutram's warm climate suddenly turn frigid, one hundred and fifty thousand years ago. Since the ground became covered with ice, the Myutram race of humankind perished along with almost all other creatures dwelling there. This glacial epoch is now only a legend, but deep down under the ice of Antarctica lay many vestiges of the ancient civilization.

Before Myutram, there existed the continent of Gonda-Ana seven hundred and thirty-five thousand years ago. During this age, those land masses which are the present continents of Africa and South America were connected, forming one huge continent. The civilization of Gonda-Ana was based on "psychic powers." One day, the Gonda-Anan continent was suddenly hit by diastrophic change, split in two and the halves drifted away from each other. And so, the Gonda-Anan civilization was destroyed by an immense earthquake with a magnitude of 10.

What I am talking about here is far from science fiction. These things actually occurred on this earth. I sincerely believe that these facts can serve as valuable references when considering the present and future civilizations.

2. The Civilization of Gonda-Ana

Throughout the three hundred million years of the history of humankind, innumerable civilizations have emerged and perished like so many bubbles floating in a river. There is no need for us to address all of the details concerning these civilizations, What we do need is information to help us ponder the present and future societies. So it is necessary to check if such information can be found in past civilizations. I have, therefore, decided to summarize the transition of civilizations, limiting my discussion to those civilizations which have existed over the past one million years, by referring to the Akashic Record of the Real World.

First of all, I will explain the Gonda-Anan civilization. The continent of Gonda-Ana was created nine hundred sixty-two thousand years ago by an eruption of a submarine volcano. This continent arose in that area of the ocean which separates present-day Africa and South America. Then, seven hundred and thirty-five thousand years ago, due to an unprecedented continental split and drift, one continent disappeared and became two separate continents.

Although four civilizations came into being on this continent, I will refer only to the last of these, the civilization of Gonda-Ana.

The Gonda-Anan civilization began some seven hundred and sixty thousand years ago, and flourished for approximately the next twenty-five thousand years, until its destruction. As I have already mentioned, this civilization was based on "supernatural powers."

The average male of the Gonda-Anan race was 2.1 meters tall while the female was 1.8 meters in height. It is interesting to note that the male had a third eye located in the middle of his forehead, about 2 centimeters above his eyebrows. The third eye, which was round in shape and of an emerald green, normally remained closed, and was only opened when the being's psychic powers were used. The female did not possess a third eye. She feared the psychic third eye of the male and eventually assumed a subordinate position.

A myth from the late period of the Gonda-Anan civilization tells that God created man and woman equally. This is evident, states the myth, because the third eye was given to the man so that he may protect himself and assure the safety of his tribe, while the womb was given to the woman so that her tribe may prosper.

At this time, the female's womb was regarded as a psychic organ through which she was able to communicate with beings in the Spiritual Heavenly Realm, and so was capable of conceiving a spirit as her own child. The would-be mother would thoroughly discuss the matter with the particular being from the Spiritual Heavenly Realm who was to become her child, and only after they had both agreed would she conceive the spirit in her. Therefore, abortion, often conducted in the present age, could not have happened during that age.

There existed eight races of people during the period of the Gonda-Anan civilization, each fighting the others for supremacy. Accordingly, these people protected themselves from foreign enemies. The third eye, then, also served as a weapon for this purpose. The color of the third eye, which was either yellow, green, purple, black, gray or brown, varied according to each race. The level of psychic development also differed from race to race.

The main power of this third eye was psychic in nature. This power is what is now referred to as psychokinesis. There were people in some races who were more concerned with the development of the power of precognition, rather than psychokinesis. Such people protected themselves by foreseeing any attack by a foreign enemy.

It is unfortunate that the importance of the mind was not taught as God's Truth during this age. These people were mainly concerned with the choice of supernatural powers they could activate and their psychic powers. This constituted their practical method of training. With the destruction of the continent of Gonda-Ana, its inhabitants returned to the Real World and formed the Sennin (superhuman) Realm, the Tengu (boastful, long-nosed goblin) Realm and the Sorcery (western sennin) Realm.

Since the destruction of Gonda-Ana, humankind has never possessed a third eye. It would seem that the chakra in the middle of the forehead, as it is so referred to in Yoga, is a remnant of this third eye.

3. The Civilization of Myutram

The Gonda-Anan civilization, which was based on psychic powers, perished due to the unprecedented, extraordinary occurrence of a continental split and drift.

This took place one autumn evening about seven hundred and thirty-five thousand years ago. As a horrifying roar came from the earth, the center of a big city known as Ecana, one of the main cities of the civilization, cracked from north to south, and in the next instant the ground severed in two. The first fault extended one hundred kilometers from north to south. Sea water seeped into this gigantic crack, indicating that the whole continent would be split in two. The second stage of transformation came three days later in the form of a tremendous earthquake. This quake, which had a magnitude of 10, was epicentered around the immediate area of Ecana. Some three hundred thousand inhabitants of the city died on that day.

The fault extended several thousands of kilometers, and the continent of Gonda-Ana slowly separated into two different continents. Tens of thousands of years after this, these continents eventually drifted apart to form the present-day continents of Africa and South America.

There was a city called Ermina in the southeastern part of Gonda-Ana where a race of people had a highly developed sense of precognition. Some of these people perceived the danger and managed to escape by sea to an uninhabited continent to the south. This is one of the origins of the legend of Noah's Ark. However, having lost the valuable tools as well as the brilliant members of its civilization, the Erminan race deteriorated into a simple agrarian society. With this change, the previously mentioned third eye also became extinct.

The most famous of the civilizations emerging on this continent was that of Myutram, which flourished from some three hundred thousand years ago until one hundred and fifty-three thousand years ago. This continent, eighty percent of which overlapped with what was to became present-day Antarctica, was named Myutram after its civilization. The earth's axis during this age was positioned quite differently than today, so the continent of Myutram had a warm climate, unlike present-day Antarctica. Thanks to this climate, these agrarian people were able to produce an abundance of a grain similar to wheat.

The dietary habits of the Myutram civilization were particularly well-developed. During this age, all possible eating habits were thoroughly studied. The relationship between diet and the human mind was pursued extensively to determine the combinations of food that would best serve the various aspects of human nature. Diversified studies were conducted on the kinds of plants that would calm the human temperament, the kinds of fish that would enhance muscular acceleration, the kinds, amounts and daily intake of dairy products that would enhance longevity, and the kinds of alcoholic beverages that would activate cerebral cells.

Doctors specialized in each area of dietary culture, including longevity, durability and the enhancement of the memory. Although they prepared for examinations differently from modern man, people studied hard from childhood in order to become such doctors.

The Myutram civilization left many findings concerning the relationship between dietary habits and the human temperament. The Gonda-Anan civilization, despite its warlike nature, attached importance to spiritual gifts, while the Myutram civilization, though peace-loving, attached no importance to spiritual matters. In other words, this civilization pioneered modern-day materialism. It was, of course, important to shed light on the relationship between diet and human nature, but since the emphasis was shifted to diet, the study and training of the soul, which was the original mission of the human being, was neglected.

Those living in the present age who take a special interest in health and beauty must have experienced several incarnations to study very hard in these subjects during the age of the Myutram civilization.

The prime period of Myutram came about one hundred sixty thousand years ago. When Moses, then called Emula (or Master Emula), incarnated on the earth, an important revolution of the mind was initiated by him with the slogan, "From life of diet to life of mind." At this time, Master Emula was severely persecuted because he ridiculed the importance of the Myutram civilization's dietary culture. Although his revolution of the mind did not succeed, he convinced people that something other than diet had a greater influence on human nature. In a sense, this was the origin of modern religions which combat materialism.

One hundred and fifty-three thousand years ago, the continent of Myutram became a frozen land mass due to a sudden polar shift. This was the beginning of the glacial period.

4. The Civilization of Lemuria

The end of the Myutram civilization was brought on by a polar shift. One evening one hundred and fifty-three thousand years ago people noticed a blood-red colored sky. Many rushed to the learned to inquire about this strange phenomenon, but no one could give any answers.

Then, at ten o'clock that evening, people noticed that the stars in the sky appeared to be moving like shooting stars. However, soon everyone realized that actually the earth was turning. Just as a ball turns completely around after resurfacing from complete immersion underwater, the earth wavered and changed positions.

Several months later the consequences of the event became evident on the earth. In the formerly warm Myutram, snow fell and the ground froze. This phe-nomenon was fatal for an agrarian civilization like Myutram and people had to fight against famine. Some tried to survive by building subterranean towns, but they perished within two or three years. Then, on the arrival of what was usually the rainy season, over five meters of snow covered the ground in a period of two weeks.

La Myut, the capital of Myutram, was completely destroyed at that time. However, as some people were able to escape by ship, a part of the civilization of Myutram survived and, consequently, formed the next civilization.

At this time only one small land mass about twice the size of the Japanese archipelago existed in the Indian Ocean. The several thousands of people who managed to escape from Myutram steadily increased in population on this land.

Eighty-six thousand years ago this same land mass suddenly began to rise and, in an instant, a continent emerged from the Indian Ocean. One year later, the entire surface area of the gigantic continent of Lemuria could be seen. This was the first time that such a huge continent rose out of the ocean. This diamond-shaped continent measured three thousand five hundred kilometers from east to west and four thousand seven hundred kilometers from north to south. This land was very fertile and was eventually covered with thick grass and dense forests.

Forty-four thousand years ago, a man who would eventually be born in Greece under the name of Zeus, emerged in this land. At that time, however, his name was not Zeus, but Elemaria. Elemaria was a genius in every field of art, including literature, fine arts and music. Just as the name for the continent of Lemuria comes from La Myut (the former capital of Myutram), so the name Elemaria was short for El Lemuria. ("El" means "the light of God"). And so, the name Elemaria originally meant "the light of God that descended upon Lemuria."

Chapter V : The Golden Age

Through the medium of art, the great St. Elemaria taught people the joy of living and the glory of God. After his emergence, the Lemurian civilization flourished in the fields of music, painting, literature, poetry, architecture and sculpture. People of the present age who excel artistically, were alive during the age of Lemuria.

After the passing of the great St. Elemaria, Manu brought an immense light to Lemuria. He was born in Lemuria twenty-nine thousand years ago. His name at that time was Margaret, and he was referred to as Master Margaret. "Margaret" means "one who competes." In this case, "compete" had two meanings : the first was because "he competed with the great St. Elemaria," who had already been respected as almighty God, and the other was because "he had each of the tribes compete in art."

Manu, or Master Margaret, was the first to incorporate the principle of competition into art. He divided the individual tribes into groups for five different arts : music, painting, literature, architecture and handicrafts. Margaret then observed as each tribe worked to the best of their abilities. Every three years a contest was held to determine the best works of art. The tribe which won the top prize in the contest came into power and governed the country for the next three years.

Although this system was limited to the arts, it was the forerunner of modern-day democracy, wherein a number of people compete with one another to determine who will govern. Furthermore, this teaching pointed out that God was the pinnacle of art and, in a sense, aimed at the unity between state and church.

Then, twenty-seven thousand years ago, the civilization of Lemuria suddenly disappeared from the Indian Ocean on an extremely hot summer afternoon while people were absorbed in the pleasure of music.

5. The Civilization of Mu

The end of the Lemurian civilization came suddenly. The Lemurians, who had mastered art, were accustomed to spending two hours every afternoon listening to music. An earthquake hit suddenly as they enjoyed themselves, chandeliers swayed violently, all of the windows were shattered and the great modern music hall collapsed instantaneously. The continent began sinking, the eastern end first.

By four o'clock in the afternoon, half of the continent had sunk into the ocean. By seven o'clock the following morning the continent had completely disappeared ! There was nothing to be seen above the blue water of the Indian Ocean but the brightly shining sun and corpses drifting on the waves. The end of Lemuria was thorough. All two million five hundred thousand inhabitants of Lemuria, whether good or bad people, vanished into the ocean.

However, the Lemurian civilization survived because the people of Lemuria had a colony. Its name was

Moa, but later came to be known as the continent of Mu.

Mu was a continent in the Pacific Ocean. It emerged before Lemuria some three hundred and seventy thousand years ago. After it was formed in the area of present-day Indonesia, Mu changed shape many times. And by the end of the Lemurian civilization, it had become twice the size of present-day Australia.

Although the continent of Mu was first inhabited several hundreds of thousands of years ago, the standard of living of its inhabitants was rather low. People in the northern part of the continent fished, those in the southern regions hunted, while those in the midwest raised cattle.

Since the Lemurians were of a prosperous and highly developed civilization, they conquered the people of Mu. About twenty-eight thousand years ago, the Lemurians formed large fleets of sailing boats and began colonizing various cities on the Mu continent. Some Mu people were captured, taken back to Lemuria, enslaved and forced to perform menial production tasks so that the Lemurians could dedicate their time to the arts. This caused a giant black cloud of disharmonious thought to form during the last era of the Lemurian civilization and, eventually, the entire continent sank on account of this situation.

Although Mu consisted of colonized cities, the Lemurian culture infiltrated the continent. After the destruction of the Lemurian civilization, the continent of Mu gradually showed signs of a new civilization.

About twenty thousand years ago, a previous incarnation of Zoroaster took place in Mu. His name at this time was Escallent, which is the origin of the word "excellent." The great St. Escallent attached much importance to the scientific application of solar energy. He classified its significance into two categories: one was "sacred light," to represent the glory of God ; the other was "practical light."

Whenever people beheld "sacred light," whether from the sun, moon or artificial illumination, they customarily joined their hands together, knelt down on one knee and bowed. This custom was the origin of that practiced in Eastern cultures where people bow to each other whenever they meet.

Concerning the second category of "practical light," Escallent was enthusiastic about the amplification of light power under the guidance of Koot Hoomy (who later incarnated as Archimedes and Newton), and also under the guidance of the scientific thinking of El Ranty in the Heavenly Realm.

People of this age obtained energy by which they lit their lamps, drove their boats and processed various materials through a gigantic solar energy amplifier which they used as a power generator. This laid the foundation of the scientific age of humankind.

In the center of the city there was a shining silver pyramid, the facets of which were regular triangles with sides measuring thirty meters in length. The solar energy was absorbed and amplified by this pyramid, and then transmitted to other pyramids with sides ten meters in length situated in the center of each section of the town. From these medium-sized pyramids, energy was distributed to even smaller pyramids with sides one meter long, which were located on the roofs of all the houses.

Pyramid power technology was also handed down to the continent of Atlantis. This gigantic amplifier of solar energy is very similar to what is now referred to as pyramid power.

6. The Age of La Mu

The Mu civilization reached its peak during the age of La Mu, about seventeen thousand years ago. La Mu incarnated in the age when faith in the sun and in the solar sciences became almighty. He was an incarnation of Shakyamuni several lives before he incarnated in India. The name La Mu means, "the great king of the light of Mu." Under his reign, the Mu continent developed into a huge empire. Although the land was originally called the Moa continent, both the continent and its civilization came to be referred to as Mu during the age of La Mu.

La Mu was pleased with the rapid development of scientific civilization on Mu and considered this to be his last chance to build a kingdom of God on earth. La Mu himself had great psychic gifts and could, of course, communicate freely with spirits in the Heavenly

Realms. The main spirits who guided La Mu from the Heavenly Realm were El Ranty and Amor, the latter of which later incarnated on earth as Jesus Christ.

The teachings of La Mu consisted of three major points. The first point was to make sure that all of the people of Mu understood that the sun was a divine existence. He taught that God is filled with light and supplies it to earthly people just like the sun. The second point of La Mu's teachings stressed that all the people of Mu should live lives of love and mercy, as does the sun. He taught that the essence of one's love and mercy was measured by how one filled others with Light. The third point was to have all of the people of Mu strive to improve themselves. Self-improvement was applied not only to the fine arts, sciences and martial arts, but also emphasis was placed on spiritual enhancement. These three points constituted the basis of La Mu's teachings.

Once you learn that La Mu was a past incarnation of Shakyamuni, who spread Buddhism in India some fourteen thousand years later, you can easily see that the origins of Buddhism exist in the teachings of La Mu.

The teachings of La Mu, seventeen thousand years ago, were the very beginning of a full-fledged religion. During the age of La Mu there was no separation between state and church. The best religion was the best form of politics and, likewise, the best man of religion made the best statesman. This point becomes crystal clear when one realizes that the human being is a separated self of God ; it is only natural that the person who is closest to God, i.e., a great man of religion, should govern the people on earth.

La Mu knelt before a shrine every night and communicated in his mind with high Divine Spirits, seeking their advice on how to manage the affairs of the state. This was perhaps the very starting point of politics. I say this because politics is a technique by which people are governed. Misjudgment by an administrator not only affects the administrator himself, but can also jeopardize the lives of the people, and can easily degrade the souls of all people. Therefore, judgment on such an important matter by the human mind is an extremely arrogant and impudent act. The very origin of politics is here. It means to be humble before God, to calm oneself, to be selfless and to hear the voice of God. Politics is to listen to the words of God.

The civilization of Mu passed its prime when La Mu died and his wife La Mentas began to govern. La Mentas was endowed both with beauty and intelligence, but since she was unable to bear La Mu's son, her political strength was weak.

Later, La Mentas was reborn in Greece as Hera, the wife of Zeus. Later still, she was born as Himiko in Japan, and then as Nyoirin Kannon in China. She recently reincarnated again as a woman in Japan and is active as a religious leader in this country.

The continent of Mu deteriorated after the death of La Mu, eventually sinking into the ocean in three different stages about fifteen thousand three hundred years ago. The gigantic modern city of La Mu, named after La Mu, also sank into the Pacific Ocean along with that continent.

Some of the Mu people, however, managed to escape. Some of them sailed northward by ship to become the predecessors of the Vietnamese, Japanese and Chinese people. Some of them traveled eastwards across the Pacific and inhabited the Andes of South America. Still others escaped to the Atlantic Ocean, in pursuit of a new world on the continent of Atlantis.

7. The Civilization of Atlantis

The civilization of Atlantis came just before modern civilization. The continent of Atlantis existed in the middle of the Atlantic Ocean, in the area of present-day Bermuda. The continent was formed seventy-five thousand years ago by the elevation of an island the size of present-day England, following the eruption of a huge submarine volcano. Atlantis became inhabited some forty-two thousand years ago by a collection of uncivilized people from the nearby islands.

Signs of civilizations appeared on Atlantis about sixteen thousand years ago, several hundreds of years before the continent of Mu sank into the ocean. At that time, the soul of a great scientist, who later would be born as Archimedes in Greece, was incarnated with the name of Koot Hoomy. He introduced the first form of civilization to these people whose main occupations were fishing and hunting. Koot Hoomy noticed the mysterious power of plants. For twenty years he studied plant growth, why stems and leaves grow, and why flowers bloom from one single seed or bulb.

He finally discovered the essence of life energy. His reasoning at that time is summarized as follows :

"Life itself is a treasure chest of energy, and a substantial conversion of energy occurs when life changes from one form to another. If we could extract the power which is generated when this energy is converted, this could become the power source for many things."

Koot Hoomy spent an additional ten years studying how to extract the power generated during the conversion of life energy and met with great success. His discovery, in fact, became the driving force of civilization.

After Koot Hoomy discovered this power source, a new light began shining in Atlantis. As the power from the conversion of life energy came to be used like present-day electricity, various devices that were similar to the electrical appliances of today, were invented. For example, each family kept a number of flasks by the windows of their houses. In these flasks were plant-bulbs to which machines were connected by thin wiring. The machines extracted the growth energy from the bulbs, and supplied it to amplifiers. In this way, each family was able to obtain the energy necessary for everyday life.

A big change occurred on the continent of Atlantis when some people who had fled the Mu continent arrived there fifteen thousand three hundred years ago. Among the Mu descendants were scientists who brought the pyramid power of the Mu civilization to Atlantis.

At this time, Grand Nyorai Maitrayer incarnated on earth from Heaven. His name then was St. Cuzanus, and he began to preach a doctrine called deism, which was a combination of pyramid power and faith in the sun. These ideas were based on the assumption that reason and science are in accordance with the mind of God, since He desires things which are reasonable and scientific.

The application of sun light typified such things as deism and was based on the following concept:

"Solar light benefits humankind scientifically through pyramid power while, spiritually, it teaches us what the mind of God is. This is how wonderful solar light is." Pyramid power was later applied to aeronautics and navigation.

Some twelve thousand years ago, the Atlantians were building a scientific civilization that surpassed that of Mu. Airship and submarine technology progressed, making use of pyramid power.

The airship at the time of Atlantis had a strange whale-like shape. It was approximately four meters in diameter and some thirty meters long. The upper half of this airship was filled with gas to keep it aloft, with the space in its lower half reserved for passengers. It could carry about twenty people. Three silver pyramids, like dorsal fins, were located on the back of the airship to supply solar energy to the propellers located at the back of the ship. The airships of Atlantis could only operate on sunny days. Passenger ships did not fly on rainy days.

The Atlantians also had submarines. These ships measured four meters wide and twenty meters long. Shaped like killer whales, these submarines were made of a special alloy. In fact, the killer whale was a symbol of Atlantis, which means "shiny golden killer whale." The Atlantian submarine was also equipped with three pyramids which looked like dorsal fins when viewed from a distance and could dive only after absorbing solar energy while floating on the ocean surface. In this way science was of supreme importance in Atlantis.

8. The Age of Agasha

Twelve thousand years ago science reigned as Almighty God in Atlantis. Around the same time, however, a certain group of conscientious people questioned the wisdom behind an extreme reverence for science. The omnipotence of science, they felt, was not necessarily in accordance with the mind of God. Rather, these people insisted that the true mind of God must lie elsewhere. Various religious reformers of different levels emerged and began preaching the way a human being should live. This period, which lasted for about one thousand years, might have been called "the age of a hundred arguments," as many theorists disagreed with each other.

Then, around this time, which was about eleven thousand years ago, Atlantis began to sink into the ocean. First, the eastern third of the continent submerged. Then ten thousand seven hundred years ago the western one-third of the continent sank, leaving only the central one-third of Atlantis above water. Nevertheless, the empire continued to exist in the middle of the ocean.

Approximately ten thousand four hundred years ago, or some eight thousand four hundred years before the birth of Christ, Agasha was born in the Atlantian capital, Pontes. This city was populated with some seven-hundred thousand people, including the royal family of Amanda which had lived in Pontes for many generations.

Agasha, whose infant name was Amon, was born as a prince of the Amanda family. When he succeeded to the throne at the age of twenty-four, Amon changed his name to Agasha. Agasha means "one who cherishes wisdom." King Agasha was later to be born in what is now Israel, as Jesus Christ.

King Agasha was a statesman and religious leader, similar to La Mu. In the royal palace stood a shiny golden pyramid-shaped shrine some thirty meters in height, where the king performed divine services.

Chapter V : The Golden Age

What was special about Agasha's reign was that during this time the citizens would gather in a huge plaza, which could hold more than ten thousand people, to hear the king preach. At that time there was a device similar to the wireless microphone.

As one may well imagine from the fact that this king was later born as Jesus Christ, the teachings of Agasha were based on "love." Although the subject matter of his preaching differed each time he gave a sermon, Agasha's basic teachings may be summarized into the following four points :

1) The essence of God is love, and the fact that we human beings are children of God can be proven by the existence of love in every person's heart.

2) To practice love, you must first love God ; second, you must love your neighbors, as they are a part of God ; and finally, you must love yourself because you are a servant of God.

3) Pray quietly in solitude and communicate with your Guardian Spirit and Guiding Spirit at least once a day.

4) The respectability of a human being is not measured by his amount of love, but by the quality of love that he gives to others. Improve your quality of love.

Agasha's teachings were admirable and his personality was deeply respected. However, a group of people who followed the deism taught by Saint Cuzanus (Grand Nyorai Maitrayer) regarded Agasha as an enemy and plotted to kill him. This occurred because Saint Cuzanus taught that God was reasonable and held science and reason in high regard, while Agasha had preached about such things as love and Guardian and Guiding Spirits, which were unscientific and unreasonable.

Those people belonging to the school of thought of St. Cuzanus believed that Agasha's teachings were misleading and gradually destroying the old traditions of Atlantis.

Of course, Agasha was certainly a Triton among the minnows and everyone recognized his noble character, but the average Atlantian had faith in the omnipotence of science and so could not believe in invisible Guardian and Guiding Spirits. Later, people from the school of deism rose in revolt, recklessly captured Agasha and other royal family members, and went as far as to bury them alive in the plaza. This scene can be compared to the end of the twentieth century because at the very same time that God's Truth is being told, evil is attempting to intervene.

Amid this horrible violence, only one of the royal family members managed to survive by fleeing from the royal palace by airship, thus escaping from the devotees of deism. This person was the oldest son of Agasha, Amon II. He fled to Egypt and became Amon Ra, and preached of religious faith in the sun. The origin of the pyramid in Egypt was the knowledge brought by Amon II.

The reckless rebels executed numerous Angels of Light incarnating on earth and it seemed as if Satan had won a victory. However, as the clouds of evil thoughts they had created enveloped all of Atlantis, the

Earth Consciousness counteracted and occurred an incredible phenomenon : the entire empire of Atlantis sank to the bottom of the sea in only one day.

Similar to many past civilizations, the end of the Atlantis civilization came suddenly. However, a group of people managed to escape by airship to Africa, Spain and the Andes of South America, where they sowed the seeds of new civilizations.

9. The Transition of Modern Civilization

After the destruction of Atlantis, civilization spread throughout the world in various forms. First, Amon II, who fled to Egypt, was worshipped there as a god and became Amon Ra, the symbol of the sun god, preaching religious faith in light. At the same time, he taught the various advancements of civilization to the Egyptian people who were mainly engaged in agriculture and cattle raising. Amon Ra's own personal pyramid, which he built as an object of worship, was the origin of the pyramids which were later constructed in Egypt.

After that, a past incarnation of Jesus Christ was born in Egypt, about five thousand years ago, by the name of Clario. Clario led the people from a standpoint that fused faith in the sun and faith in love.

On the other hand, in South America, descendants of the civilizations of Mu and Atlantis were cooperating to build another unique civilization. These people regarded extraterrestrial beings as gods and based their own civilization on communication with these beings. They even devoted themselves, for a period of time, to building landing bases for spaceships in the Andes mountains so that spacemen could land on earth.

Seven thousand years ago, a king by the name of Rient R. Craud was born in Inca, in the Andes mountains. He declared that the extraterrestrials were not gods. Craud preached the mystery of the world of the mind and taught that God did not exist externally, but at the bottom of everyone's heart. He professed that the purpose of human life was to search for the mystery of the world of mind. According to Craud, it was important for a human being to bring himself closer to God by refining his own mind.

Rient R. Craud was a reincarnation of La Mu of the Mu continent and was later reincarnated in India as Gautama Buddha, or Shakyamuni, and there preached Buddhism. Unlike four-dimensional or five-dimensional human spirits, a nine-dimensional spirit is a huge mass of light energy and does not transmigrate into the life of a single person, but rather a part of its energy descends to the ground. This is also the case for Jesus Christ.

Three thousand and seven or eight hundred years ago, Zeus was born in Greece. He excelled both in academics and art, as is apparent from the fact that people considered him to be both omniscient and omnipotent. Since Zeus was engaged in general artistic endeavors in the ninth dimension, he gave rise to the glorious Greek culture. He was cautious with religion so people would not be distressed with feelings of guilt, and instead he concentrated on how to make humanity cheerful and free. As a result, gods in Greek myths are very cheerful and lively beings.

Three thousand and some hundreds of years ago, Moses was born in Egypt as the child of a slave and set to freedom afloat a raft of reeds in the Nile river. Fortunately, Moses was rescued from amongst the reeds of the river bank and raised in the Pharaoh's palace. When he grew up, Moses realized that he was a child of a slave and, in time, led hundreds of thousands of people across the Red Sea and established what is now Israel.

Moses received a variety of divine revelations. The famous, "Ten Commandments," were communicated by El Ranty, and "Genesis," of the Pentatuech, was received from a nine-dimensional being later named Shakyamuni Buddha.

Finally, about two thousand years ago, Jesus Christ was born among the Israelites. He preached about love, and after he was crucified, he appeared before his disciples : the phenomenon known as "the Resurrection," which was actually the materialization of Jesus as an astral body. In order to convince his disciples, of the reality of the phenomenon, Jesus dined with them. The fact that Jesus later ascended to heaven apparently shows that this was not the resurrection of Jesus in the flesh. The beings in heaven who guided Jesus were

Buddha, El Ranty, Moses and Michael.

In the Orient, on the other hand, two thousand five hundred years and several decades ago, Shakyamuni taught Buddhism in India, while Confucius taught Confucianism in China. Thus, the seeds of the laws were sown in various parts of the world and have grown to create modern civilization.

10. Toward the Golden Age

Looking back through the nearly one million years' history of civilizations until the current civilization, we notice that there are certain aspects which are common among all of them. These can be summarized into the following five points :

1) Every civilization experiences periods of glory and decline.

2) God sends Great Guiding Spirits of Light to each civilization.

3) When civilization reached its peak and was shining with its last light, demons intensified their activities and caused clouds of dark energy to shadow humankind. Catastrophic events occur in such forms as the shifting of the earth's axis or the sinking of a continent.

4) New civilizations usually seek different sets of values, while inheriting some of those from old civilizations.

5) However, there were no exceptions in the fact that

all civilizations provided an environment for the soul training of human beings in the process of their transmigration.

If you consider the modern civilization, with reference to these five common elements, the present age—the latter half of the twentieth century—looks surprisingly similar to the end of the Mu and Atlantis Civilizations. The reasons are : this age is leaning toward the omnipotence of science, and materialism is prevalent. People's minds are in chaos and social evils are rampant. And although misleading religious teachers are thriving, genuine religious leaders are emerging in many areas of the world.

Comparing the consequences of the past civilizations with the current state of modern civilization, Its future seems rather clear. As the modern civilization covers not only one continent but the entire globe, catastrophes will involve the whole world. Moreover, it is highly probable that such a catastrophe will take place in the coming decades.

Based on the above, it is easy for me to speak like a prophet. I can visualize the cataclysms which will take place on the earth and the destiny that awaits humankind.

However, I must tell you this : no matter how big the catastrophes that will take place, the world will not end. Every civilization experienced such a situation and it always seemed that the world would end. However, humankind never failed to build a new paradise of hope, a new civilization filled with Light.

Just as the individual human being transmigrates from one life to another, so does humankind and civilizations. In other words, civilizations on the earth are recurring. Therefore, I would like my readers to keep the following words deep in mind : *The end of one thing is the start of another.*

The very reason I am writing this book, *The Laws of the Sun*, receiving revelations from the nine-dimensional Cosmic Realm, is because the time is close at hand for the entire earth to sink into darkness and at that time we will need a beacon. We will need the Light of God's Truth. This very book, *The Laws of the Sun*, is the rising sun of God's Truth , and a light for the new civilization to come.

Humankind will usher in a new civilization in the twenty-first century after decades of extreme chaos and devastation. The new civilization will begin in this land in Asia. It will spread from Japan to Southeast Asia, Indonesia and Oceania. Some of the existing continents will sink into the ocean, and a new continent of Mu will rise from beneath the Pacific Ocean to offer a stage for a new civilization.

Parts of both Europe and America are also destined to sink into the ocean. However, Atlantis will rise again, and become an even larger continent than before. Jesus Christ will reincarnate on that continent around the year 2400. Then, around the year 2800, the Great Guiding Spirit of Light, Moses, will reincarnate to build a new cosmic civilization on the continent of New Gonda-Ana, which will re-emerge from beneath the Indian Ocean.

Among the readers there must be people who will reincarnate and listen to the teachings of a revived Jesus or Moses. These future civilizations will only become possible if we let the sun of God's Truth rise here and now in Japan. When the world sinks into darkness, Japan will shine as the sun. From this point of view, those who are born in this age are the chosen people, to whom many missions have been assigned.

Many of those who helped spread God's Truth during the ages of La Mu, Agasha, Buddha and Jesus are alive in Japan today. There are many living Angels of Light in the world, some of whom are in Japan. I am sure that some of them are included among the readers of this book.

Chapter VI
Roar Like a Lion
•

Roar Like a Lion

•

1. Open Your Eyes

My readers, we are not existences that have reincarnated on earth merely once or twice. Having looked back through the history of the past million years in Chapter V, we saw many peaks and declines of civilizations and continents. Were the people who lived in those civilizations completely different from us? Did they appear out of the blue?

Actually, we are the very ones who lived as the people of Atlantis and Mu. In the store of memory at the bottom of our souls we have recollections of transmigrations in the past tens or hundreds of civilizations. These are the memories of the soul, which is given to all humankind, and do not only belong to a special group of spiritual people. However, humans have forgotten the wisdom acquired through eternal transmigrations because we live in flesh.

In reality, flesh is merely a vehicle in which the soul carries out its training in this world. Therefore, you yourself are not a vehicle but a driver. I would like you to awaken to the part of you that manipulates your body, and encounter your true self.

It would be a gross mistake to assume that you could understand everything about the world only on the basis of the knowledge you have acquired in school for ten or twenty years. No one could dare to teach you your true self unless you search for it on your own.

In order to find your true self, you must first comprehend the truth of the soul by throughly researching your mind. "Enlightenment" means to find your genuine self. It means that you can describe your true mind with your own words and declare that, "This is me."

I regard the human soul as a part of God, and the art of God's self-expression. However, with the freedom to create and act, human beings live self-indulgently, imitating the monkey in a Chinese tale, "A Travel in the Occident." Without realizing it, humans have forgotten their parent God, and the mind of God, and lead lives at the mercy of selfish desires and evil passions. Human degradation became definite when they became more attached to this world on the ground than to Paradise in the Real World. Consequently, in the other world, humankind created a world of desire and struggle that is identical to the earth ; namely, the Hell Realm.

To know yourself is to know that you are a child of God ; it is to know the mind of God. And to open your eyes means to awaken to and study your spirituality and the existence of the Real World beyond the third dimension.

If you are satisfied with the current state of your life and your view of human existence, you may remain asleep. If you truly wish to awaken, however, you should begin researching your mind. There awaits you the key to the Kingdom of God.

2. Abandon Your Attachment

To know your genuine self, you must abandon your false self. And to do so one must be prepared to abandon that negative aspect of your being. The false self consists of :

1) A Self That Takes Love from Others

First is the self which thinks of nothing but taking love from others. God offered the Cosmos. He gave us human souls and human flesh. God also gave the sun, air, water, the Earth, ocean, animals, plants, minerals and all other things without expectation of anything in return.

While living in a world which was "given," why do humans think only of taking from others ? Having been given so much love by God, how much more do humans need to be satisfied ? Only those who do not know God's Love take love from others. But what exactly is the love which you want to take?

Is it money, position, honor, fame or title? The words, "I love you from the bottom of my heart?" Or the words, "I owe everything to you?" Or an apology from a person who insulted you? Sexual services? A body nicer than the one given to you by your parents? Words of praise about your child or the academic achievements of your husband? Is it to hear compliments about your beauty or handsome face or cosmetic technique? Are these the sorts of compensation and words of praise that humans need?

Of what good are such things? How do they help you to improve yourself? Such self-love builds a wall separating you from others and, eventually, a wire fence like the kind at a zoo will stretch across the entire world. People don't realize this because they cling to the wrong values and cannot realize their own faults. It is impossible to attain true happiness when one has a mind that adheres to wrong values.

2) A Self That Does Not Believe in God

The most pathetic are those who do not believe in God or the world that God made. Those who think that human beings are born accidentally as a result of sexual intercourse and, therefore, are living their own separate and individual lives ; there are the most pitiful selves.

Those who dare to say, "I cannot believe in God

whose existence cannot be proven," are already judging God. They are so conceited to believe that they can judge God. A human being cannot prove the existence of the God, who has been in existence since long before man first appeared on this earth. The proof lies in the next world and will be shown to humans after death. At that time it will be too late because such people will be placed into complete darkness and become so confused that they will not be able to prove even their own existence.

3) A Self That Does Not Make Efforts to Search for the Way

The third false self is an ego which makes no effort to search for the way. Examples of such an ego are, first of all, one who is lazy-hearted ; secondly, one who does not study God's Truth ; thirdly, one who views others unfairly ; and finally, one who is prejudiced.

God expects humans to make eternal efforts. Therefore, those who do not make efforts cannot claim to be children of God.

Are you making efforts and deepening your study of Truth everyday ? Can you truly appreciate the ability or true value of others ? Are you living free of prejudice ? Prejudiced people can never improve themselves or study the truth of the soul. Lack of prejudice is a virtue in itself, and is in harmony with the mind of God. To argue without listening to the opinions of others is proof of prejudice.

4) A Self of Attachment

The false self is attached to many things. To know one's genuine self is to live everyday based on the mind of God and to know that this world is a temporary realm for training one's soul. You will eventually return to the other world no matter how attached you are to this world. Human life is in transiency and may end suddenly at anytime. Therefore, one must live a day as if it were a whole life. No one in Heaven is attached to the earthly world. Every one in Hell, on the other hand, is strongly attached to this world. We must keep this fact in mind.

3. Glow Like Red-hot Iron

To become unattached to worldly things is a drastic measure for a human being but will ensure happiness in one's eternal life. Discarding this attachment, however, does not mean that one should live passively or negatively. Rather, the very act will lead to a positive and active life.

Look at the people around you. Do you notice how weak the people with attachment appear. What makes a person attached to his position, fame or income? What compels a person to be attached to the name of his school or company? What causes a person to be attached to the act of showing off or other such forms of vanity ? What is good about attachment to such matters ? What is the benefit of being highly praised by the people of this world ? From the viewpoint of God, whose existence is greater than the vast macrocosm, how ephemeral, vain and trivial human attachment to worldly things appears ! Can you understand this ?

Only when you glow like red-hot iron, abandoning all worldly attachment, are you living a genuine life. That is the true way to live as a child of God. It is a life of which God approves.

A human being cannot return to the other world after death with any position, honor or wealth acquired in this world. One's title in this world is of no use in the next. How many former Japanese prime ministers do you think are suffering in Hell in the next world ? Hundreds or even thousands of presidents of respectable companies have fallen into and are now suffering in the Hell of lust, the Hell of struggle and the Hell of beasts. Are you aware of this fact ? If a man, who is only good at earning money, indulges in sexual pleasure with many women and finishes his life in the same way he lived, do you know how many hundreds of years he must suffer in Hell to compensate for his several decades of pleasure ? Hell is not merely a myth of old, or an expedient way to scare people away from evil, it actually exists.

Through the eyes of a person who has mastered the Truth, those agonizing in the other world can be seen more easily than goldfish in a glass bowl. Their most common trait is that the more attachment they had to this world, the greater their agony.

The mind is the essence of the human being, which is actually a soul. Therefore, nothing but your mind can take you back to the other side after death. The mind is everything. Only after realizing this fact can you assume a firm stance in life.

If your mind is the only thing with which you can return, you have no choice but to return with a beautiful mind. Of course, a beautiful mind is the mind that God would praise. It is full of love and is giving, nurturing, forgiving and appreciative. In order to return with such a mind, we must first glow like red-hot iron in refining and purifying our minds.

What is the opposite of attachment? The answer is love, because, to love means to give. There is absolutely no attachment in love that constantly gives to nurture others.

In short, to abandon attachment, we must first give love. What have you done for your parents, to whom you owe so much? What have you done for your brothers and sisters? Have you been able to meet the expectations of your teachers? What have you done for your friends? What have you done for the people that you have encountered through the will of Heaven in the course of your life? What have you done for your neighbors? What have you done to your girlfriend or boyfriend? What have you done for your wife or husband? How much of your parent's efforts do you recall when you raise your own children? Could you forgive those you hated? Have you helped calm the anger of others? How much of God's Love have you reciprocated by living your life with courage?

4. Life is a Daily Battle

Having sworn to live as children of God, given up worldly attachments and opened up our minds, what then are we supposed to do?

It is clear that we must not retreat to the mountains, stand under a waterfall or spend days meditating. Human beings were not born to live as hermits in the mountains. Nor were we born to fast. Shakyamuni proved the futility of such acts in obtaining enlightenment two thousand five hundred years ago in India. So that Shakyamuni's life is not meaningless, we must realize that enlightenment cannot be attained through such physical hardships.

A genuine key to enlightenment cannot be found either in a life of extreme pleasure, or in physical training that tortures the flesh. The Middle Way that abandons these two extremes is the kind of life which God expects us to live.

Even though the true nature of a human being is a mind and a soul, I do not mean for you to disregard your body. Your body is a precious vehicle for training in life and has been given by God through your spiritual relationship with your parents.

There are people who lovingly polish their cars everyday. If you can take care of your car, why not take better care of your own body. Maintain good health through appropriate exercises and balanced nutrition. You have to sleep well and lead a regular life. You should refrain from too much alcohol, which can upset human reason and intellect. It is acceptable to take alcohol occasionally, for refreshment. However, if you become dependent on alcohol, you will gradually loose reason, become controlled by demons of Hell and eventually loose your body to them. It will inevitably lead to failure in your work and a collapse of your family.

Although it is so easy to say that you should enter the Middle Way and abandon both extremes, it is hard to put this into practice. The deeper you think about the Middle Way, the further it extends. Then, how can you come to live life in the Middle Way ? How can you obtain the proper scale by which to measure this Way ? This is the next question people will ask.

To enter the Middle Way, we require two scales. One is the scale of self-reflection based on the Genuine Eightfold Path. The other is the scale of self-observation based on the Theory of Staged Develop-ment of Love. I would like you to live your life with these two scales.

The Genuine Eightfold Path teaches people to see, speak, work, live and think rightly, make right efforts, have right intention and concentrate one's mind rightly. It is the method by which to correct extreme sways of both mind and action, based on "rightness," and to identify the Middle Way. One can get along with others and lead a harmonious life only if he takes the Middle Way. However, you should avoid the danger of being reduced to living a passive and pessimistic life by being involved in too much self-reflection based on rightness. Constant reflections tend to halt your life.

If you have managed to reflect sufficiently, the next step is to express it in mind and action. In short, it will be a practice of appreciation, that goes beyond saying "Thank you" to others. The very nature and a true practice of appreciation is more positive. It is to ask oneself, "What on earth can I do for others ?"

It is the love that perpetually gives. It is to practice love with appreciation and without return. Therefore, it is essential for you to ask yourself if you are in the stage of the "love that loves," the "love that forgives," or if you have reached the stage of "love as existence"; to gage your own progress. The Development Stages of Love are reliable scales that show your daily progress.

"Reflection" and "progress" are two scales by which to prove that you are living as a child of God. You must, therefore, reflect everyday, refrain from extreme thoughts and actions and check your daily progress. This is the way to win the daily battle of human life.

5. Brilliant Life

Life requires "reflection" and "progress." However, I think that satisfying only these makes a life rather colorless; it is important to have "brilliance" in one's life. I would like to answer the question, "What is brilliance?"

Brilliance is at the moment when a light radiates its illumination. I think the moments of brilliance can be categorized into three:

The first moment of brilliance is when one has recovered from an illness. Illness is a trial in life and one's humanity is tested by how he struggles through it. Illness can be regarded as a trial in two senses: First, illness accompanies a physical affliction; and second, it is also a mental affliction.

As for the physical affliction, it is generally caused by either a lack of a regular life, overwork or a problem with your thoughts. Therefore, the one who is suffering from physical illness must realize his mind is equally suffering. And he must reflect on the reasons why his body is ailing.

Eighty percent of illnesses are accompanied by some sort of haunting evil spirit. In many cases, spirits of the dead are suffering through the patient's body; these spirits are sweating through the agony at the same time as the patient. The proof is that the moment when haunting spirits are exorcised, the patient's high fever drops dramatically and he gets up immediately, feeling refreshed in body and soul. This shows how susceptible a body is to spiritual influence.

Reflection and appreciation are most annoying to the haunting spirits. When a patient starts to reflect and appreciate, he radiates a halo from the back of his head. His vibration changes so that it becomes too uncomfortable for the haunting spirits who possess him. To intensify the halo, the patient has to solve his own mental difficulties.

To solve these difficulties, he has to review and eliminate his attachments one by one. Ironically, when a patient manages to get rid of all his attachment and is ready to die, the light of the Truth shines down with the help of his Guardian and Guiding Spirits in the other world and his condition quickly improves. This is the moment of a miracle. Those who have experienced such a miracle have undergone a major conversion and started a new life. And this brilliance will not only brighten up the saved person, but will also become the light of the mind that illuminates other people.

The second moment of brilliance is when one has awakened to religious faith. The difference between a life with faith and one without is as great as the difference between a person who gropes in the dark and one who carries a lantern.

This three-dimensional world is certainly that of materialism. However, if one becomes obsessed by materialism, regarding it as truth, he will gradually pursue only pleasures, or devote himself to struggle. In other words, he will become the most pitiful sort of person who has forgotten the eyes of God. Religious faith is a ray of light which brightens up a road of darkness. Only this light can open the eyes of a person who is blind to the Real World.

The third moment of brilliance comes when a person opens his Spiritual Path. It means opening up the door of his mind to become able to communicate with his Guardian and Guiding Spirits in his subconsciousness. Spiritual Path differs from so-called supernatural powers or psychic ability. In contrast to these abilities which are obtained through extraordinary training or innately, the Spiritual Path can be acquired "a posteriori" (learned in the course of one's life). What is wonderful about this Spiritual Path ability is that everybody who is practicing God's Truth can acquire it. All ancient men had this ability before Hell was created. Modern people have simply forgotten this fact.

It is not difficult to open your Spiritual Path. If you can clear your mind like the ancient people, every one of you would be able to communicate with spirits in the multi-dimensional worlds. The best way to make your mind clear is through reflection. Human beings have lost their natural brilliance of soul through the influence of their environment, education, thoughts, habits and the six kinds of obsession derived from the eyes, ears, nose, tongue, body and thoughts. To regain brilliance, there is no other way but to remove the "blurs of mind" known as mistakes which you make yourself. For this purpose, Right Concentration is necessary ; to concentrate and reflect on every single act and thought you have had since your birth. Then comes an encounter with God's Light through your open Spiritual Path. This is exactly the third moment of brilliance in life.

6. Time is Precious Like a Diamond

To live a powerful life, it is essential to spend the limited time rightly. A human soul can only reincarnate once in several hundreds, or even thousands of years. His earthly life is a very precious experience. In spite of this, most people idle away their time without seeking a deep meaning of life. What a waste !

Even though you finally perceive the existence of God, awaken to the faith and want to start your life anew in the last stage of your life, you can not recapture the time that has already passed like an arrow or a flowing river.

Fortunate are those who awaken to God's Truth at an early stage of life. It will be best if they can live the rest of their lives in accordance with God's Truth. Of course, encountering Truth at a late stage is not in all respects meaningless. If you are determined to live a full life, it will be a splendid one.

There is a secret for life ; to meditate at the moment of your death. I advise you to occasionally consider what you will think and how you will feel on your death bed. If you can think, "I am glad I have lived" or "Life is truly wonderful," you are the one who has lived a happy life.

On the contrary, there are people who cannot help regretting how they lived. How pitiful those people are ! They will have to reflect upon their own lives in front of high grade spirits in the other world after death. As if they are watching a television, their own lives will be projected on a screen in the presence of a big audience.

A person who has just returned to the other world after death will be decisively reminded of what sort of human being he was from the viewpoint of God. There will be no room for lies or excuses. He will know where he should go, judging from the audience's eyes. Those who must go to Hell will do so willingly because, after realizing what sorts of people they were, they will be too ashamed to live in paradise. Viewing from the perspective of physics, their spiritual vibrations are too coarse to match the finer vibrations of the other people. It could also mean that their conscious form has become so three-dimensional and so materialistic that its gravity is too heavy to stop the people from sinking.

Some people, however, receive applause from the audience, when their lives are reviewed after death in the Real World. At the moment they realize the mistakes of their lives, shed tears and beg for God's forgiveness, the audience of the other world will applaud loudly, pat the shoulders of new comers and shake hands. The Angels of Light rejoice with tears when the scene of that person who risked his life for the mission work of God's Truth is projected.

These are the scenes that await you in the future. This moment will come without fail. Therefore, it is essential that we all live our lives, keeping in mind the moment of death, or rather, always asking ourselves whether we could die tomorrow without regret.

If you continue your life as it is now, won't you be ashamed on your death bed ? Won't you regret ? How will you judge yourself based on your conscience ?

It is necessary to change your awareness and viewpoint in order that your entire life may shine like a diamond. Reflect on the way you have lived up to now, imagining the moment of your death. It will be exactly the same as reflecting from the viewpoint of a good willed third party. That is the key to lead a life which is as precious as a diamond. That is the secret for living a full, brilliant life.

7. You Must Have A Dream

To have a dream in life is essential. A life without a dream is a life without hope. It is, of course, important to reflect upon the evils you have created and resume good intentions. However, I think it would be unsatisfactory to merely balance the total of life at zero by eliminating the negative elements.

To have a dream is to design a life that is as splendid as possible. For example, when an architect builds a house he first draws a blueprint, then has carpenters build the structure in accordance with his design. In the case of our own lives, the architects are no one else but ourselves. Therefore, unless we draw a good plan, the outcome will be unsatisfactory. If you are so keen to have the proper plan for a house, why not make a good plan for your own life? Failure to do so is to live life blindly. Too many people live their lives by leaving everything to chance.

By the way, you don't need to think too seriously about the plan. Essential is whether or not one has or can visualize a dream. There is a big difference between the people with a dream and those without, in terms of how confident they are in life. It makes a big difference when trying to influence other people.

You feel happy when you meet a person who has a dream. It makes you feel that you should help that person and that you, too, must do something on your own.

"Having a dream" is something that intoxicates people. I don't believe there has ever been a person without a dream who is still remembered now for his great work. Born as a human and living in this world, it is extremely important to have the pride to live a big life. Living one's life within a small realm is not modesty.

Modesty is only necessary while one is in the process of enlarging his own capacity. Modesty is needed only because one is fully confident in the way he lives. Modesty is like a brake ; brakes do not make a car advance. It is an accelerator that is most necessary to move a car forward. A car does not function without an accelerator. A brake is provided for the reason of safety. It is installed to prevent the car from going out of control and to avoid accidents.

I have warned you many times against descending into Hell. But you will never achieve improvement merely by praying everyday in fear of going to Hell. You must step on the accelerator. If you think you are going too fast, step on the brake. The brake exists for that purpose. If you are living a positive life of progress, you must check to see if the brake is broken. If you are certain that you can reflect immediately when making a mistake and correct the course of your life then step on the accelerator with full force. This is the meaning of having a dream and realizing it.

The advantage of having a dream is not only in drawing a plan ; it has another mysterious function. A dream is a continuous vision in the mind. It will eventually be communicated to the Guardian and Guiding Spirits in the other world, or the Real World. Guardian and Guiding Spirits are always concerned about how they can lead the people of the Ground Realm. However, most of the people living on the ground have only transient thoughts, without any concrete target of life. They are not even sure what sort of life they want to live.

What sort of guard or guide can these people expect ? Revealing everything to earthly people from the beginning will spoil their initiative to live a positive life. What the Guardian and Guiding Spirits are allowed to do is to give inspiration to living humans. Usually, that is all they can do.

In the case of a person with a firm dream though, the only thing the Guardian and Guiding Spirits should be concerned about is how to help person to realize his dream, by giving appropriate inspiration. Therefore, if you are successful in having a concrete dream and visualize it, there is a great possibility for the dream to come true with the help of the Guardian and Guiding Spirits in the other world.

In fact, this is self-actualization in a true sense. To achieve a goal of self-actualization, you must first have a dream, visualize it, pray to the Guardian and Guiding Spirits for its realization and eventually it will come true. It is needless to say that you must be able to improve your own personality and at the same time make other people happy through your dream.

8. Have Golden Courage

Courage. Is it only I who gets excited with this word ? The word courage reminds me of a broadax driven into a huge tree. It makes me hear crisp sounds which echo in the early morning woods like vigorous beats of life. I think we humans can fell big trees named trouble in life, only because we have this broadax named courage.

So, when you are about to give up on life or are miserable and depressed, please remember that God granted us broadaxes named courage.

A human being arrives blind in this world. He has to grope his way while depending only on his five senses. And for this reason, God granted us at birth a broadax named courage and said, "Go and cut your way through the woods of destiny." Thus, all of us carry this broadax at the hip. Why do we not realize this? Before complaining about pains and asking others to solve your problems for you, or before claim ing to be sad and asking others for sympathy, why don't you cut the string of destiny that binds you with the broadax of courage? The Chinese Zen Buddhist monk, Mumon Ekai, tells the following story in his Zen Koan book, *Mumon-Kan* (literally, *Gateless Barrier*):

"Human beings have forgotten that they are end-owed with a great power, and are paralyzed by worldly common sense, the opinions of others, and what doc-tors say. As a result, they think themselves to be material human bodies, which are at constant risk of breakdown. However, a genuine self is a child of God, and is infinitely powerful. If you are successful in experiencing Cosmic Consciousness through Zen medi-tation, your genuine self or your spiritual body will become huge like a giant looking down at the earth under his feet. Just by stepping on the earth, he can shatter into sprays of water this three-dimensional galaxy, which is only a pool of water in the high-dimensional universe. And the human's spiritual worlds, which are also called the fourth or the fifth dimension, will be found so far below that you will have to lower your head to see them."

It seems that this monk, Mumon Ekai, had acquired the enlightenment of the Nyorai Realm. When one attains such enlightenment, he realizes that a genuine human being is not a spirit so tiny that it can dwell comfortably in a body, but an energy body which can expand to be as large as the Cosmos. When such a person meditates, he feels that his body is expanding just as he views the Earth far below him.

Originally, the human being was an unrestricted existence endowed with great power. Now this same human being is restricted by three-dimensional senses, school education and public common sense. He also restricts himself, believing that there is no spirit and no life after death. When he becomes ill, he becomes a pitifully trivial existence that continually says that he does not want to die.

Summon your golden courage and cut down the huge tree of delusion with your golden broadax. Wedge in your broadax with strength. Conquer your agony, suffering and hindrances of destiny with your courage. Sever the threads of destiny that bind you by summoning your golden courage.

9. Never Give Up

Courage is important. When one summons his courage, he realizes that he is a man of great power. Even a person who, upon realizing that he has great power, rises from his sickbed and begins leading a powerful life, or a person who is awakened to God's Truth by overcoming the delusion of materialism, may be losing his vigor once he is tempted by three-dimensional human beings as a result of continually receiving vibrations from the three-dimensional material world.

This is the very moment that one must clench his teeth and persist. It is similar to running a marathon. Sooner or later a moment of torment will come when you are tempted to drop out of the race. Giving up at this point, you would have no chance to win or even complete the race.

Once you are through this difficult moment, your feet will feel light and you will be able to complete the race. Many of you must have had similar magical experiences. The same thing happens when swimming. If one continues to swim at the very moment when he wants to stop, clenching his teeth despite his shortness of breath, he will suddenly feel his body become one with the water and be able to go on swimming like a wave.

Of course, life is not a marathon or swimming race. However, life has moments when you have to endure pain. And once you are through such difficult times, you will acquire confidence and feel closer to the Light of God.

Personally speaking, I had such a period as well. Born in the countryside and rather simple, since primary school I always thought, "Because I am dumb, I will only equal the others with two or three times their efforts. In order to become a man who can contribute to the world, I have to use every moment to try four or five times harder than others, even while they are asleep."

I can remember myself of ten years old studying until very late at night, with a blanket around my lower body and gloves on both hands, deep in the mountains in Shikoku—I didn't have any heating system. When I look back on my teenage years I find that I was like a tortoise and not smart and brilliant like a hare.

This rural boy arrived at Tokyo station in the spring of my eighteenth year, with a bag packed with more than thirty kilograms of books. Although it was still freezing cold, my cheeks were red and I was perspiring. I was at a loss as to how to get to Shibuya station. That spring, I applied to the number one group of the liberal arts division of the University of Tokyo, but failed a secondary examination. The following year though, I managed to slip in thanks to one year of perseverance.

However, I was soon victimized by my inferiority complex when I compared myself to the other law students in the University of Tokyo, who were selected as the elite from all over Japan. As a result, I was prone to boasting. Detesting myself for behaving like that, I then suffered from anthrophobia (the fear of people), shut myself in my room and became absorbed in reading.

From the winter of my sophomore year until the following summer, I remember writing love letters to an attractive, brilliant urban girl. Half a year after I began sending her letters, I finally got a reply written on a single sheet of paper. With her letter in my hand, going up the stairs to my second floor boarding house, I felt discouraged with this letter so thin that sunlight could go through it ; I had been sending her love letters in parcels !

I talked to her only once. Because I was more erythrophobic (fear of blushing) than anthrophobic, I could only say a word or two to young ladies before I found myself too embarrassed to continue talking.

Even during those disappointing days, I kept reading like a tortoise. I even cut down the amount I would eat for dinner in order to keep my brain sharp while I studied law and politics. However, even after one extra year at the University, I failed the essay test of the state law examination though I passed the short answer test. I also failed in the examination to become an upper-grade state public service official. Moreover, I tried to stay in the university as a teaching assistant, but the door was closed because my academic performance was too weak. Eventually, I managed to be hired (or more accurately, picked up) by a general trading house.

Recalling myself at age ten, studying in the cold, deep in the Shikoku mountains, breathing on white gloves to warm my hands and with cold, flushed ears, I shed tears. Every time I tried to attain worldly success, my hope was destroyed. And, looking back on my false life up to that point, I thought as follows:

"Alas, I haven't returned anything to society. I have lived my life according to my own will to become a mere villain. If I die now, I will agonize for hundreds of years in the deepest bottom of Hell."

In the winter of my twenty-fourth year, I read the books written by Keiko Takahashi, *The True Genesis— Hell version, Heaven version* and so on, which led me to *The Discovery of Mind*, written by Shinji Takahashi. Darkness is always the deepest before the dawn and destiny hits the bottom before it brightens up. Eventually, my wheel of fortune began to turn. This was before my graduation, in the final examination period.

10. Roar Like a Lion

After having studied nothing but law, I encountered the "Right Law of God's Truth" instead of the six codes of law. Then, in January of 1981 I began reading a volume called *God's Truth* out of Shinji Takahashi's Trilogy, *The Discovery of Mind*. When I reached somewhere around page 57, I realized that my heart was beating very quickly and my body began to sway back and forth.

Something was bound to happen. I kept reading the books one after another by the same author and found myself always saying, "I already know this Truth. I have learned it before."

On the twenty-third of March of the same year, a Sunday, I was suddenly struck by the feeling that somebody was trying to speak to me. I hurried to get a card and a pencil. My hand which held the pencil started to move as if it had its own life and wrote, "Good news, good news" on one card after another. When I asked who it was, it signed "Nikko"; It was the Buddhist monk Saint Nikko.

After a while, St. Nichiren started to send messages. His first teaching to me was in the three phrases, "Love others. Nurture others. Forgive others." At that point, I thought I had been a monk of the Nichiren Sect in my past life.

Finally, a decisive moment arrived. It was an evening in June of 1981. A voice as solemn as I had never heard before suddenly echoed in my heart. A person named Shinji Takahashi started to send messages to me. He had passed away five years before, I had never met him personally while he was alive, nor had I been aware of his existence.

Takahashi : "Ryuho Okawa, I came here to tell you of your vocation. You must teach the laws of salvation to save humankind."

Okawa : "My Master, I'm only an ordinary business man at a trading house. I am even a freshman at that. What do you think I can do ? Or, do you mean that I should cooperate with the GLA (God Light Association), the body which your daughter has succeeded from you ?"

Takahashi : "GLA does not need you. You have to clear your own way. You have to go your own way."

At that time, the spirit, named Shinji Takahashi, told me what my vocation was and who I was.

The person most surprised by this story came rushing from my home town. It was Saburo Yoshikawa, the current Advisor to The Institute for Research in Human Happiness. Then, in the same month, June, 1981, Jesus Christ spoke to Saburo Yoshikawa through myself. It was a very shocking event.

Since then, Yoshikawa and I have been researching God's Truth, sometimes being surprised at or wondering about innumerable spiritual phenomena unfolding one after another in front of us. In the meantime, St. Nichiren informed us that Mr. Yoshikawa was St. Nichiro in his past life, one of Nichiren's six senior disciples. St. Nichiren also revealed that he was acting as my guardian spirit through that relationship.

At the same period, spirits in heaven began to appear in response to my calls. Considering the vital importance of the matter, we remained silent for four years before we became convinced that these spirits were the genuine high-grade spirits. No matter how much we doubted, the words they spoke were true, and absolutely full of much more dignity and wisdom than any intellectuals on the ground could speak.

In August, 1985, we presented our first publication of communications with the spiritual world, *Spiritual Messages of St. Nichiren,* for public judgment. We were elated that the reaction was much greater and the criticisms much fewer than we had expected. As more of our books were published ; *Spiritual Messages of Kukai,* in October ; *Spiritual Messages of Jesus Christ,* in December ; *Spiritual Messages of Amaterasu-O-Mikami,* in February, 1986, the response from readers grew bigger and bigger.

While publishing these spiritual messages, I continued to work for the trading house. I was in charge of international finance in one of the international general trading houses in Tokyo. I also worked in its New York headquarters for training, and took courses at New York University. Without realizing it, I began to think about the ordinary success of my career, leaving Saburo Yoshikawa most of the work of publishing spiritual messages. I was gradually climbing up the corporate ladder in the company, and became quite popular with women in the office.

Eventually, in June, 1986, I was struck a hard blow. Saint Nichiren, Jesus Christ, Ame-no-Minakanushi-no-Mikoto (the Lord God of the Heavenly Center, principal god in Japanese Shintoism), Amaterasu-O-Mikami (the Sun Goddess in Shintoism), Moses and Shinji Takahashi descended one after the other and sternly advised me to immediately leave the company.

After three sleepless nights, I finally tendered a letter of resignation to the company. And on the fifteenth of July of that year, I formally resigned the trading house I had spend some years with, just after I had turned thirty on the seventh of July.

In September, 1986, I established "The Institute for Research in Human Happiness" in Tokyo and have dedicated my whole life to spreading God's Truth. I hear the voice of Jesus Christ echoing, "If a grain of wheat does not die...." I intend to roar like a lion during the remaining decades of my life. And I pray that there will be as many people as possible who will roar with me for God's Truth.

Epilogue

It has been only three years since the original Japanese edition of this book, *The Laws of the Sun* was published. However, the thought revealed here has spread like wildfire all over Japan. This organization, "The Institute for Research in Human Happiness," based upon the principal ideas described in this book, has come to count its members in the tens of thousands. Or rather, with the international distribution of this English edition, this number is expected to grow to well over a million.

I earnestly desire for people around the world to become familiar with this thought of salvation which represents the new Japan, and attain true happiness. It is my firm belief that the day will surely come when people all over the world are awakened to their true existence as children of God, and work hand in hand for the happiness of humankind and for the creation of Utopia on earth.

Ryuho Okawa
May, 1990

Table of Dimensional Structures

Dimension	Name of Realm	Substructure	Development Stage of Love	Name of Spiritual Being
Ninth	Cosmic Realm (Sun Realm)		Love of God Love of the Messiah	Grand Nyorai, Guru
Eighth	Diamond Realm (Nyorai Realm)	Sun Realm	Love as Existence	Nyorai
		Light Divine Realm		
		Semi Divine Realm		
Seventh	Sacred Heavenly Realm (Bosatsu Realm)	Bonten Realm	Love that Forgives	Bonten
				Bosatsu
Sixth	Godly Realm (Light Realm)		Love that Nurtures	Arahan, Syoten-Zenjin
Fifth	Spiritual Realm (Mental Realm. Goodman's Realm)		Love that Loves	
Fourth	Posthumous Realm	Astral Realm	Love of Instinct	
		Hell Realm	Love that Deprives	
Third	Ground Realm (Earthly Realm)			

GLOSSARY
OF
TERMS

Akashic Record :
Records of the entire history of humankind which are stored in the Real World.

Allah :
The Moslem name for God : Creator.

Angels of Light :
Spiritual beings of the upper sixth dimension and higher. In Buddhism, they are called Shoten-Zenjin (Special Mission High Spirit), Bosatsu and Nyorai.

Arahan (Arahat in Sanskrit) :
A state of enlightenment or a spiritual being in the upper six-dimensional Godly Realm.

Ashura Realm :
Hell ; a realm of strife and destruction, lacking tranquillity and harmony.

Astral Travel :
Out-of-the-body experience ; the astral (or spirit) body resid-

ing in the flesh leaves the body and visits the Real World.

Aura (Halo) :
Circular light emanating from the back of an enlightened person's head. Angel's ring of light. Visible only through spiritual sight.

Bonten (Brahma in Sanskrit) :
A state of enlightenment or a spiritual being of the upper stage of the Bosatsu Realm (the seventh dimension), and the lower stage of the Nyorai Realm (the eighth dimension).

Bosatsu (Bodhisattva in Sanskrit) :
A seven-dimensional spiritual being. A Bosatsu has achieved self-perfection and devotes his life on the ground to loving and serving others. He helps the Nyorai teach the Laws of Truth.

Buddha's Nature (Buddhahood) :
Divine nature. The true nature of a child of God. All sentient beings and all creation are the manifestations of God's Will and are God's wisdom.

The Code of Manu :
An Indian (Continental) law book, written in verse with a literary flavor, which was compiled in approximately the 2nd century B.C.. It covers a broad range of principles starting from everyday customs to religious and moral conduct. Regarded as the base of various law books of later ages.

Core Spirit & Branch Spirit :
Occasionally called spiritual brothers. Spirits lower than the seventh dimension are composed of groups of six souls in order

to facilitate soul discipline. Each spirit consists of one core spirit and five branch spirits, each of which reincarnate alternately to engage in soul training.

Divinity :
This is comprised of the primordial God and spirits stationed above ordinary people (high spirits, advanced spirits).

Dualism of vice and virtue :
The view that both good and evil exist, and that the world is where the two conflict with each other.

Enlightenment :
Another name for the true happiness which can be applied both to this world and the other world. It is the greatest happiness that God has ever given humankind. It is to fully understand the true nature of humans and the world that God created as well as the purpose and mission of human life.

Experience of Cosmic Consciousness :
A state in which one is unified with the Universe. Only those who are in the upper realm of the eight-dimensional Nyorai Realm can attain this state of enlightenment.

Garden of Eden :
A paradise described in the Old Testament. Adam and Eve, who arc said to be the first man and woman, were expelled from this paradise after being duped into eating the forbidden fruit by the devil who appeared in the form of a snake.

Garden of Gethsemane :
Olive garden in Gethsemane in the suburbs of Jerusalem.

Noted as the holy place where Jesus Christ prayed on the night before he was arrested.

Genesis :
The first book of the Old Testament. The contents are the Creation and the history of humankind beginning with the first man on earth, Adam, through approximately twenty generations, until his descendant, Joseph.

God's Truth :
Simply, the Truth. The true teaching which emanated from God conveying His Will. "God's teaching" transcends any individual religion.

GLA (God Light Association) :
Buddhist-based religious body founded by Shinji Takahashi in 1969. After the founder's death in 1976, the body was succeeded by his eldest daughter, Keiko Takahashi.

Grand Nyorai, Guru or Grand Guiding Spirit of Light :
Other names for saviors from the nine-dimensional Cosmic Realm (Sun Realm). They refer to Shakyamuni, Jesus Christ, Moses, Confucius and so on, who are outstanding figures in the history of humankind.

Guardian Spirit :
A spirit in the other world, who is assigned to lead a person undergoing soul training in this world. Every person is allotted one Guardian Spirit without exception. Usually a spirit with a close spiritual relationship with a certain person serves as a Guardian.

Guiding Spirit:

Advanced spirit who instructs those who are engaged in especially important missions on the ground. The Guiding Spirit has a higher spiritual grade than the Guardian Spirit of a living human.

Han-nya Shin-gyo (Prajna Paramita Hridaya Sutra in Sanskrit):

A text which simply describes the essence of the Prajna Paramita Sutra (one of the Buddhist scriptures).

Inca:

An American Indian tribe which founded the Incan Empire which prospered in the Peruvian Highlands in South America.

Infinite Hell:

The Hell located in the deepest part of the other world where go the politicians, religious and social leaders who mislead the public.

Japanese Shintoism:

The religion of Japanese origin with Amaterasu-Omikami as the supreme goddess. It extols the virtue of order and courtesy.

Kan-Jizai (Unrestricted Vision):

A Divine Power of the level of enlightenment above "Nyo-shin." Also refers to a supernatural power which is attainable by high spirits called "Bonten."

Kapila Castle:

The castle at Kapilavastu, where Shakyamuni was born and

lived for 29 years until he left his family.

Karma :
Characteristics of souls which are formed in the course of transmigrations.

Koan :
Metaphysical questions serving as objects of Zen meditation. It indicates the depth of their views and insight.

Kushinagara :
The village where Shakyamuni passed away. The capital of the kingdom of Malla which existed in central India.

Kyoto School :
A sect of philosophy that appeared in Japan in the beginning of the 20th century. It tempers European philosophy with oriental concepts such as Zen. Kitaro Nishida was a philosophy instructor at the school.

Lesser Vehicle (Hinayana in Sanskrit), Greater Vehicle (Mahayana in Sanskrit) :
The Lesser Vehicle refers to the Buddhist teaching or training emphasizing self-establishment or cultivation of oneself. Only after having mastered the Lesser Vehicle stage can one advance to the Greater Vehicle stage which emphasizes helping others or the salvation of humankind.

Lust Hell :
A Hell where go those who indulge especially in sensual desires.

Matter is void, void is matter :
A phrase from the *Han-nya Shin-gyo* (see the explanation in this glossary). It aptly explains the relationship between matter and energy ; namely, energy creates matter, which can be again converted into energy. It symbolically illustrates a cyclical manifestation of God's Light energy.

Middle Way :
The way for humans to live as preached by Shakyamuni. This reflects the idea that the true way of living lies in abandoning extremes.

Mumonkan :
A book written by Mumon Ekai explaining his understanding of classic Koans (refer to the explanation of Koan).

Nazareth :
A town in Galilee of present-day Israel where Jesus Christ was raised.

Nirvana Sutra (Nehan-Kyo in Japanese) :
One of the Buddhist scriptures, which describes the events during the period when Shakyamuni entered Nirvana (peaceful passing).

Nyorai (Tathagata in Sanskrit) :
Eight-dimensional beings. (Broadly speaking, the Grand Nyorai of the ninth dimension are included.) Archangels of Light. As God's representatives, they teach fundamental ideas which are the foundations of cultures and civilizations.

Nyoshin :
A stage of enlightenment. A state of mind of the seven-dimensional Bosatsu Realm and the eight-dimensional Nyorai Realm.

Past life (Former Life) :
Refers to the life time before the present life. There is a presupposition that man reincarnates again and again, namely, reincarnationism.

Powertron :
A spiritual device which absorbs and amplifies the Light of God ; Angels of Light have these in their chests.

The Pentatuech :
The Five Books of Moses; the first five books of the Old Testament, which are "Genesis," "Exodus," "Leviticus," "Numbers" and "Deuteronomy."

Pytron :
A spiritual device in the Real World which multiplies human souls.

Reformation :
The 16th century movement to reform Christian beliefs. This upheaval spread quickly throughout Europe. Its main contention was to consider the Scripture the ultimate authority and criticize the Roman Catholic Church. Eventually, this caused a split of the Christian Church into the Protestants and the Catholics.

Right Law :
Genuine teachings that flow from God: God's Truth.

Rojin :
One of the Six Supernatural Powers. Although gifted with high-level spiritual abilities, a person with this power can live as ordinary people.

Seicho-no-Ie :
A Japanese religious body established in 1930 by Masaharu Taniguchi.

Sennin Realm :
A realm in the other world that is inhabited by those who have mastered spiritual powers through research, but lack the ability to give love to others.

Seven Colors of Light :
The Light of the primordial God is divided into seven colors, each representing one of the various attributes of God.

Shikoku :
The smallest among the four main islands that form Japan. Located in the south-west region of Japan.

Shoten-Zenjin (Special Mission High Spirits) :
Angels of Light in the upper six-dimensional Godly Realm who give guidance to the leaders of every special field in the sixth dimension or leaders on the Earth.

Sodom and Gomorrah :
A legendary town described in the Old Testament. It is said

that the town was destroyed by God because its people indulged in excessive sensual pleasures and homosexuality.

Sorcery Realm :
See Sennin Realm.

Spiritual Grade :
The extent to which one has evolved, spiritually, toward God. One's spiritual grade is roughly described by the current "dimension" to which one belongs.

Spiritual Path :
A "spiritual passage" through which a man on earth communicates with spiritual beings in the Real World. If this communication is manifested as spiritual speech, conversation and so on, it is called a Spiritual Path phenomenon.

Tao :
Literally, "the way." Approximately the same as enlightenment, though it is more symbolic.

Taika Revolution :
A coup d'etat which occurred in the middle of the 7th century in Japan and the subsequent major political reformations. This laid the foundation of centralized control of the later governments.

Teleportation :
Instantaneous transportation of matter to a distant point.

The Ten Commandments :
Ten disciplines that were given to people by God through

Moses as stated in the Old Testament. They demand that people dedicate themselves to only one God, observe the Sabbath and respect their parents. They prohibit idol-worship, abuse of the name of God, murder, adultery, theft, false witness and covetousness.

Tengu Realm :
A realm in the other world which is inhabited by those who are conspicuous with their spiritual powers. Those beings lack the ability to love others freely.

The Third Religious Boom :
Japan's social phenomenon in which, since the 1970's, many religious groups have come forth that are characterized by their Doomsday theories and mysticism. Young people who are interested in psychic power or supernatural phenomena are main supporters of this fad.

Unshakable Mind :
The state of mind which is unfettered by any worldly trouble, but is peaceful and tranquil and always directed toward God.

Waters of Bermuda :
Located in the western Atlantic Ocean; where the Continent of Atlantis once existed.

World of Real Existence, or the Real World :
The "other world" which is usually contrasted with "this world." The World to which all human beings go after death. It is invisible because it is the world of thought.

Yoga :

A traditional Indian Method of disciplining both mind and body. Basically aims at heightening spirituality, but some schools of Yoga emphasize physical training.

Zen :

A training practiced by Zen sect Buddhists. By performing Zazen (literally, sit-down meditation), they concentrate the mind, bring it into harmony and then attempt to purify it by eliminating the dark thought accumulated in it.

GLOSSARY
OF
CHARACTERS

Amaterasu-O-Mikami (The Sun Goddess) :
(c.8 century B.C.) The supreme deity in Japanese Shintoism. She reincarnated in Takachiho-no-kuni (the unified ancient Japanese nation in Southern Kyushu) as a daughter of Izanami-no-Mikoto and Izanagi-no-Mikoto, his wife, and became the first queen in the nation. Although she was not from the ruling Family, she was named heir to the throne by spiritual instruction which she followed in leading the nation to prosperity.

Ame-no-Minakanushi-no-Kami (The Lord God of the Heavenly Center) :
(c.9th century B.C.) Believed to be the Absolute God of Creation in Japanese Shintoism but actually a political and religious leader who established a nation called Takachiho-no-kuni in Southern Kyushu in Japan. Governed it according to the teaching of "Monism of Light."

Ame-no-Tokotachi-no-Kami :
(?) The fifth patriarch of Takachiho-no-kuni, the nation founded by Ame-no-Minakanushi-no-Kami (The Lord God of the Heavenly Center).

Amida Nyorai :
In the Japanese Jodo (Pure Land) and Jodo-Shin (True Pure Land) sects, he is worshiped as the principal Buddha in the "Western Pure Land," with many of his teachings are recorded in various sutras. He once reincarnated on the ground, embodying part of Jesus Christ's consciousness.

Ananda :
(?) One of the Shakyamuni's ten major disciples; renowned for memorizing the sermons; a cousin of Shakyamuni. After Buddha's death, he recited the sermons which were later compiled as a collection of sutras.

Apollo :
(c.2600B.C.) Son of Zeus; after his father's death, he began to receive revelations and spiritually lead the people of countries that battled with neighboring countries. At the center of his teaching is the idea of God as Light. He reincarnated embodying part of the consciousness of Chief Archangel, Michael.

Archimedes :
(c.287—212B.C.) Greek mathematician and physicist, born in Syracuse (Sicily); founded the science of hydrostatics with so-called Archimedes' principle.

Calvin, John :
(1509—1564) French theologian, ecclesiastical statesman and one of the most important Protestant Reformers of the 16th century. Calvinism influenced the development of Protestantism in many parts of Europe and North America.

Confucius :
(552—479B.C.) Sage of ancient China; China's greatest philosopher and political theorist. The teachings of Confucius were transmitted to all later generations through the *Lun-yu* (Analects of Confucius).

Dainichi Nyorai (Mahavairocana in Sanskrit) :
The buddha worshiped in the esoteric teaching and the most important buddha in the Shingon sect; the embodiment of the reality of the universe. Dainichi means "great illumination."

Dogen :
(1200—1253) The founder of Japanese Soto Zen sect; a disciple of one of Eisai's successors. He studied in China and then taught the importance of Zen meditation, self-reliance and ascetic spiritual training in Japan.

Eisai :
(1141—1215) The founder of Japanese Zen sect (Buddhist). After studying Tendai (T'ien-t'ai) teaching, he went to China twice and brought the teaching and method of Rinzai Zen (meditation). He also introduced the cultivation of tea into Japan.

Gabriel :
One of the Archangels of Jewish, Christian, and Muslim tradition. In the New Testament, Gabriel is the angel who announces the birth of Jesus to Mary. In the Muslim religion, Gabriel is believed to have dictated the Koran to Mohammed.

Hera :
(c.17th century B.C.) Wife of Zeus and a goddess in Greek

mythology.

Himiko or Himuka :

(c.200) Japanese queen who unified 34 small regions in Northern Kyushu into a nation called Yamato-no-kuni (The country of great harmony). Her rule was characterized by the spiritual guidance she received and the use of female aids for political advice. After she passed away at age 38, the country invaded Central Japan and established the Imperial Government, the forerunner of the present Imperial Family.

Honen :

(1133—1212) The founder of Japanese Jodo (Pure Land) sect (Buddhist). He taught that everybody could be saved by reciting the name of Amida (Buddha).

Ippen :

(1239—1289) The founder of Japanese Ji (Time) sect, commonly called "Wandering Saint." After studying Tendai (T'ien-t'ai) teaching, he followed Honen's teaching of reciting Homage to Buddha for salvation.

Jesus Christ :

(4B.C.—29A.D.) Jesus of Nazareth, the founder of Christianity, whose deeds and message are recorded in the New Testament.

Kanmi-Musubi-no-Kami :

(?) The third patriarch of Takachiho-no-kuni, the nation founded by Ame-no-Minakanushi-no-Kami (The Lord God of the Heavenly Center). He reincarnated in Japan embodying a part of the consciousness of Chief Archangel, Michael.

Kukai:
(774—835) The founder of Japanese Shingon sect (Buddhist). He studied in China and received the teaching of esoteric Buddhism. His main concern and activity was the spiritual salvation of the public. Posthumously entitled Kobo Daishi.

Lao-tsu:
(587B.C.—502B.C.) Chinese philosopher and founder of Taoism (The Teaching of the Way). He emphasized simplicity, naturalness and spontaneity in all the essentials of human life.

Leonardo da Vinci:
(1452—1519) Italian artist and scientist. Master of arts of painting, sculpture and architecture, accomplished engineer and pioneer investigator of the natural sciences at the time of the Renaissance.

Luther, Martin:
(1483—1546) German Augustinian friar; the leader of the Protestant Reformation. He inaugurated the movement called Protestantism, which shattered the external structure of the medieval church and at the same time revived the religious consciousness of Europe.

Maitreya (Miroku Bosatsu in Japanese):
(?) One of famale disciples of Shakyamuni. Later her name became known as a Bosatsu to succeed Shakyamuni as the future Buddha. Belief in Miroku Bosatsu prevailed in India around the beginning of the first century A.D., and spread to China and Japan.

Mani :
(215—275) Persian religious teacher and founder of Mani-cheanism. He taught the doctrine of the dualism of good and evil. He took ideas from Buddhism, Christianity, Gnosticism and Zoroastrianism; known as the "Apostle of Light."

Manu :
(?) The reputed author of the most renowned law book (*The Code of Manu*) of the ancient Hindus in India. In several passages of the Vedas as well as the Mahabharata, Manu is mentioned as the progenitor of the human race.

St. Mark :
(?) One of the twelve apostles of Jesus, about ten years younger than the Master, also the writer of the second Gospel of the Bible.

Michael :
The Chief Archangel described in the Bible. Kami-Musubi-no-Kami, Martin Luther and Apollo are his spiritual brothers.

Mohammed (Muhammad) :
(570—632) The founder of Islam. Born in Mecca and became a merchant; his trade brought him into contact with Judaism and Christianity. At the age of 40, he had a vision of the Archangel Gabriel, recorded the teaching of Allah in the *Koran* (the Muslim sacred book), emphasized the importance of strictly regulating everyday life according to the teaching of the only God, Allah.

Moses (Mosheh in Hebrew) :
(c.1350—1250B.C.) Hebrew prophet, teacher and leader who

delivered his people from Egyptian slavery and founded the religious community known today as Israel, based on a Covenant relationship with God.

Mo-tzu :
(438—395B.C.) Chinese philosopher, preached universal love and pacifism (Moism). Later Moism was lost due to the politics of China.

Mumon Ekai :
(1183—1260) Chinese Buddist monk who compiled various Zen Koans (refer to the explanation in this glossary) into a systematic whole and dedicated the work to the Emperor of the period. He clarified the meaning of Zen meditation and emphasized the importance of severing each moment from the rest with the aspiration for enlightenment.

Myoe :
(1173—1232) Revered as a restorer and priest of the esoteric Kegon sect in the Kamakura period in Japan; a disciple of Eisai and the founder of Kozanji temple in Kyoto, Japan.

Newton, Sir Isaac :
(1643—1727) British physicist, philosopher and mathematician. Regarded as the most prestigious of modern times. Discovered calculus, formulated the theory of universal gravitation and laid the foundation of modern science.

St. Nichiren :
(1222—1282) The founder of the Japanese Nichiren sect (Buddhism) who preached and practiced Hokkekyo (Lotus Sutra), severely criticized other sects and the Kamakura

Shogunate and was exiled.　Later he was pardoned and dedicated himself to writing and teaching.　One of the greatest Japanese spiritual leaders.

St. Nichiro :
(1245—1320)　One of St. Nichiren's six senior disciples.

St. Nikko :
(1246—1333)　One of St. Nichiren's six senior disciples.

Nishida, Kitaro :
(1870—1945)　Japanese philosopher, professor of Kyoto University; regarded as the authority of the idealistic philosophy of European tradition; also famous for his philosophy of "nothingness" in the Japanese way.

Nyoirin Kannon :
In traditional Buddhism, commonly believed to be a female deity attendant of Amida Nyorai.　A Kannon (fulfilling people's wishes) Bosatsu with "wish-fulfilling jewels" and a "wheel" representing the Law.

Plato :
(427—347B.C.)　Greek philosopher; one of the most brilliant figures in the history of Western philosophy.　Plato was a young associate of Socrates and left many works on Socrates' life and dialogues.　Plato established a school for research, the Academy, the first university.

Rahula :
(?) The son of Shakyamuni and Yashodhara.　One of Buddha's ten major disciples.　He was respected as the foremost incon-

spicuous practitioner.

Rennyo :
(1415—1499) The restorer and reformer of the Jodo-shin
(True Pure Land) sect in the Muromachi period in Japan.
He founded a seminary in Yoshizaki, Echizen for dissemina-
tion in the Hokuriku district on the Sea of Japan.

Saicho :
(767—822) The founder of Japanese Tendai sect (Buddhist),
studied in China and returned to Japan with the teaching of
"one path for everyone to reach salvation." He was later
involved in a religious controversy.

Shakyamuni :
(654—574B.C.) The founder of Buddhism. Born to King
Suddhodana and Queen Maya in Kapilavastu, North India,
he was called Siddhartha and also Gautama. He attained
spiritual enlightenment and was called Buddha ("the enlightened one").

Shariputra :
(?) One of the Shakyamuni's ten major disciples, known as the
wisest. Born as a brahmin's son, he first followed Sanjaya
Belatthiputta. He died of an illness a few years before Shakyamuni's passing.

Shinran :
(1173—1262) The founder of the Jodo-shin (True Pure
Land) sect. He became Honen's disciple and propagated the
teachings of "nenbutsu" based on Amida's power. He wrote
the foundation text of the Jodo-shin sect.

Shotoku Taishi:
(574—622) Prince Shotoku, the second son of the Japanese Emperor Yomei. He became the Prince Regent and assisted Empress Suiko. In 604, he promulgated the Seventeen Article Constitution. He encouraged Buddhist studies and founded many temples. He is regarded as the father of Japanese Buddhism.

Shuddhodana:
(?) The king of Kapilavastu in North India and father of Shakyamuni. He first opposed his son's desire to renounce the world, but when his son returned to his home after being enlightened, Shuddhodana was converted to Buddhism.

Socrates:
(c.469—399B.C.) Greek philosopher and moralist. He was the first of the great trio of ancient Greeks—Socrates, Plato and Aristotle—who laid the philosophical foundations of Western culture.

Swedenborg, Emmanuel:
(1688—1772) Swedish scientist, theologian and religious mystic. After winning recognition as a natural scientist in 1745, he began receiving spiritual revelations and left numerous books about the exploration of spiritual worlds.

Takahashi, Shinji:
(1927—1976) Japanese religious leader, the founder of GLA (God Light Association). A successful businessman in his secular life. He began to receive revelations at age 40, then taught the basic principles of Buddhism, and emphasized the importance of reflection, taking the Middle Way and regulat-

ing one's mind and actions. Through many demonstrations of the "spiritual path" phenomena, he revealed the truth of the laws of transmigration.

Taniguchi, Masaharu :
(1893—1985) The founder of Seicho-no-Ie, a spiritual movement based on the theory that all religions emanate from the Primordial God. He revitalized Japanese Shintoism and introduced American "New Thought" philosophy to Japan. His many works include, *Seimei-no-Jisso* ("Truth of Life").

T'ien-t'ai Chih-i :
(538—597) The founder of the Chinese T'ien-t'ai (Tendai) sect. His name and title were taken from Mt. T'ien-t'ai, which was a center for the practice of Chinese Buddhism. The Tendai teaching was brought to Japan in the middle of the eighth century.

Upali :
(?) One of Shakyamuni's ten major disciples, known as the foremost observer of the precepts. He was of humble origins, having formerly been a barber at the court of Kapilavastu. He joined the Order at the same time as Ananda.

Yakushi Nyorai (Bhaishajyagusru in Sanskrit) :
Literally, a "Buddha of Medicine"; the Buddha of the Land of Emerald in the east; a high spirit who helps people with medicine or the Buddha of Healing. Recently, a part of this spirit was reincarnated as Edgar Cayce (1877 - 1945) in the United States.

Yasa, Yasas, or Yasoda :
(?) The son of a wealthy merchant in Varanasi who eventually became Shakyamuni's disciple. Yasa was Buddha's first convert after the five ascetics.

Yashodhara :
(?) The wife of Shakyamuni before he renounced the world, and the mother of Rahula. She later became a disciple of Buddha.

Yoshikawa, Saburo :
(1921—) The advisor to The Institute for Research in Human Happiness.

Zeus :
(17th century B.C.) King of ancient Greece, later considered to be the chief deity and Almighty God in Greek mythology. Born in Mycenae, married to Hera; later fought against and defeated his brothers, Poseidon and Hades, and unified the whole of Greece.

Zoroaster (also, Zarathustra) :
(6th or 7th century B.C.) Persian religious teacher; the founder of Zoroastrianism which includes belief in an afterlife and the continuous struggle between the universal spirits, good and evil.